The Apples Under My Tree

Margaret Barnes Heath

Copyright © 2015 Margaret Barnes Heath

All rights reserved. This book or any portion thereof may not be reproduced in any form by electric or mechanical means including photocopying, recording, or information storage whatsoever without the express written permission of the author.

ISBN::-10:1512228893
ISBN-13:978-1512228892

DEDICATION

I dedicate this book to my beloved children who brought smiles and happiness to the family.

Thanks to,

Bill, John, Bud, Scotte, Diane, and Terry.

CONTENTS

	Acknowledgments	i
1	Bill	1
2	John	27
3	Bud	39
4	Scotte	101
5	Diane	125
6	Terry	158

Preface

I knew my children had memories of their childhood that I knew nothing about, because I was too busy to observe them, or they were of a mischievous nature. I approached my grown children with a tape recorder, and informed them they were protected by the statute of limitations, and could not be prosecuted for their actions. Many interesting and funny stories were revealed.

I am proud of the fruits of my labor. I don't feel it was luck that produced these fine capable young people, but hard work on my part and theirs. Their father and I showed them the way, and provided an environment conducive to learning, and growing into productive adults. We encouraged individuality; problem solving, imagination, and creativity. Strong work ethics expanded their talents. We showed them the joy in helping others, and giving back to the community. They were raised to be independent.

We planted our roots in the fertile soil of Maine, and I believe this was a big factor in their development. My duty was to nourish them, protect them from ill winds, defend them from storms, and to comfort them in times of distress.

As my branches become brittle with age, my children in turn offer protection for me.

All of them are known for their big smiles and twinkling, blue eyes.

Bill is independent, self-employed, enjoys problem solving, and using his hands.

John was a serious, serene young man that impacted his community.

Buddy displays his great humor, smiling face, hard work, always busy, and caring for others. His leadership abilities have grown, he enjoys a challenge where he has to find a solution, and he mentors the young.

Scotte is a master of music and art. She is compassionate and has always had a love of children. Her frugal life style made it possible for her to take an early retirement, and enjoy life.

Diane is meticulous, organized, determined, and hard working. These qualities lead her to owning her own business of designing and crafting beautiful stained glass pieces of art. She will always be a beautiful princess.

Terry used her passion for sports to become an excellent field hockey coach, a committed teacher, and a mentor. She maintains friendships with many of her school peers, and they still have their annual canoe trips.

The fruits of my labor have produced loving, devoted, hardworking adults which are the apple of my eye. I could not be more proud.

Acknowledgements:

Thanks to Scotte Barnes for her poem,

Karen Hawkins for her thoughts,

Gail Bell for her song about John and

Carol Noonan for her song about Captain C'ete.

Bill

Childhood

Bill was my first born; I was determined not to spoil him by holding him all the time. He grew up to be a very independent, self-reliant child. He did not want to be held for story time, but sat in one corner of the couch, and waited for me to read the story.

He was an adventurous baby, climbing the stairs at a very young age. I didn't carry him down the steps, but made him come down one leg and one arm at a time. That training took about three days.

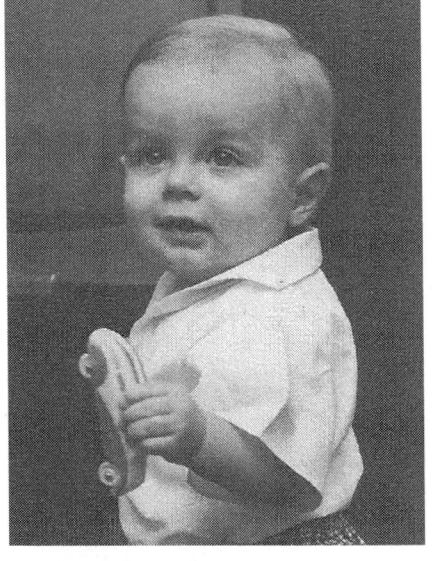

He had just turned four when we arrived in Maine. This was a whole new experience for all of us. He loved the out-of-doors, and playing in the snow. It took longer to bundle him up, than the time he spent playing outside. One day he was impatiently waiting for me to help him put on his boots; he sat on the floor, and tried to dress his feet by himself. Patience was not one of his virtues, and as he twisted and tugged at his boots, I heard him exclaimed, "Damn it."

My attention quickly turned to him, and I told him we didn't use that word.

His innocent eyes looked up at me and he explained, "I mean the beaver kind of dam."

Bill tells:

We moved to Maine when I was a little four-year-old boy. Frequently, early in the morning my parents took my brother, John, and me to the woods to pick raspberries for jam. Dad carried my eighteen-month-old brother on his shoulders, and John reached out and picked berries which he stuffed into this mouth. They thought that was so cute. I had more important things to do. There was exploring that needed to be done, rocks to be over turned, and I wanted to splash in puddles.

My dad commanded, "I want to see some berries in your pail, or you won't get any jam this winter!" That was when I learned my dad was a man of his word. I had no jam on my toast the entire winter. The next summer I picked berries before I explored.

One thing I learned as a kid growing up was a strong work ethic. It is something I see lacking in kids today. I appreciated the jam, and I made sure I did a good job before I was paid. Today's kids expect to be paid adult wages, and they do not appreciate it.

Billy was a good eater. He ate anything, but as a small child he preferred to play outside rather than eat. He ate his meat first; rather he put the meat in his mouth, and parked it in his cheeks like a chipmunk. Then, he ate the rest of his meal, excused himself from the table to go play, and chewed his cud as he played until it was gone. He knew I did not permit snacking between meals, so if he was hungry he knocked on a neighbor's door, and charmed the lady by saying, "You know you're the best cooker in town," whereupon, he was invited in for a glass of milk and a cookie. What a charmer.

Bill tells, "Because I had to eat everything on my plate, it caused me trouble later in life. I was just as strict with my daughter, Jennifer, and made her eat all her beets; she still holds it against me to this day. I learned, at times, we have to do things in life that are uncomfortable."

I asked Billy to tell me some things he remembered as a child.

I was kind of a loner, because I was three years older than my brother, John. I played by myself inventing, and making my toys.

I remember knocking out my front teeth. Several times I threw rocks in the air, and watched them come down hitting me in the face. I didn't have front teeth for two years. I guess that makes me not the smartest kid on the block, but I quickly learned about gravity.

My best friend was my imagination. My parents purposely did not give us many toys; they wanted us to broaden our imagination.

My story of Bill's accomplishments:

As a child Bill's greatest assets were his imagination and craftsmanship. He didn't have many toys, so he built his toy-of-the-day from scrap wood, and other discarded bits and pieces of things he could find. He was all boy! He loved to take things apart, and sometimes he put them back together. Any time a new bike showed up, he had to take it apart to see how it worked. He took the fenders off trying to make it lighter. He oiled, greased, and checked the bearings.

Heavy snow atop a barn's roof caused it to collapse, damaging the boats stored below. Doc purchased, and refurbished one of the smashed boats.

Five-year-old Billy watched the repairs, and then constructed a motor for his wagon using some boards about six inches square, and nailing them together to form a box.

He attached some knobs, a long three inch board with two thin three by one-half inch shingles tacked as a cross for the propeller, and binder twine for the starting rope. With pride he clamped his first creation to his wagon.

Billy was ready for an imaginary fishing trip. He tied a length of clothesline to the porch pillar, and threw the other end into his *boat*. He found a stick for his fishing pole, and tied binder twine to one end. Not wanting to get his feet wet he stepped from the porch into his *boat,* and using the sturdy fishing pole, he pushed away from shore to spend the morning adrift, repeatedly casting for multicolored *leaf/fish.*

When I called him for lunch he pulled the clothesline rope hand-over-hand until he reached shore arriving with dry feet.

A few weeks later his dad bought a chain saw. Billy quickly removed the propeller and used a saw to cut away the square corners where the propeller had been until it resembled the cutting bar on the chain saw. The knobs were changed and I heard, "Hurummmm, hurummmm, and I knew he was happy with his conversion.

Bill tells the following:

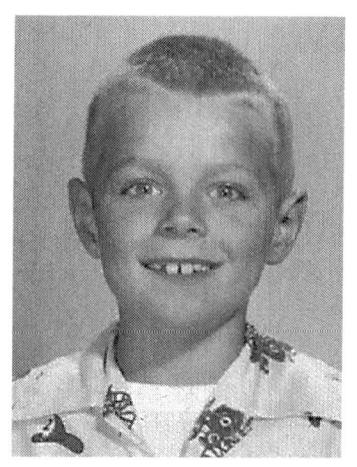

My favorite television show was *Sea Hunt* with Lloyd Bridges. I made my own back-pack using scrap pieces of pine boards, ropes, and two tomato juice cans. The other kids had only one oxygen tank. Before the show started I put on my scuba tanks, and then sat in front of the television set ready to go on expeditions with them.

I was six years old when Dad came home with a small two-wheeled bicycle. He spent a couple minutes teaching me how to ride it, and then he had to go into the house to take care of patients. I was so tickled with my new bike. I rode it up to Shot Gun Alley to show my friend, Jim Sargent. Jim was the old fellow who skinned my weasels when I caught them in my traps.

I did a good job pedaling up the road. I was careful to ride on the edge of the main road, but when I arrived at Jim's I realized I didn't know how to stop, so I ran into the back bumper of Grandpa Harry's car. The front fender was a little banged up. I brought the bicycle home, hid it by the wood pile, and covered it up with a piece of metal roofing so nobody knew what I had done. I didn't ride it for a couple weeks. Mom and Dad were so busy they didn't notice.

Some of my recollections:

When Billy was about five years old he was playing in the neighbors rotting apple tree on a sunny winter day. A large branch of the tree broke off, and pinned him in the snow. He struggled to get out, but the branch held him in place. He started screaming for help. Finally, Dad heard him, and came to his rescue. The neighbor lady banned Billy from her property.

About four years later he was in her yard shaking loose the fence posts that held the snow fence upright. He had Slick, the constable, at his side. The story about this dastardly deed started when the men who plowed the snow, wanted to push the mounting snowbanks back, and the snow fence was interfering. They went to the road commissioner who intern went to the selectmen. After studying the problem they decided the town owned the land twenty feet on each side of the middle of the road, and the fence was on town property. They ordered the road commissioner to remove the fence, but he was scared of the neighbor lady, so he requested the presence of the constable to handle the irate neighbor in case of trouble. Billy found out what was going on, and he gladly assisted the road commissioner.

The day came when Billy entered kindergarten. I put Baby Buddy in the old wicker buggy, which I bought at an auction for a quarter, and held the hand of four-year-old John as we walked across the bridge, and on until we came to the school house hill. Billy helped me push the buggy up the steep incline.

We were greeted by the teacher, and Billy took his seat at a desk. John and I sat on the small first grade chairs with Buddy on my lap. The bell rang, and class opened with the reciting of the pledge of allegiance to the flag. As I stood holding Buddy I realized I was still wearing my apron. Holding him in front of me I tried to crumple up the apron, and tuck it between Buddy and me.

Bill tells another story:

My mom and dad always encouraged us to learn and use new words. When I started kindergarten I heard some new words I had never heard before, and I was anxious to share them with my mother even though I didn't know what they meant. She grabbed me by the arm; turned me to face her and sternly said, "I don't ever want you to use those words. They are not nice words, and we don't talk like that!" Believe me I was a fast learner following that one-sided conversation, and I never used those words again.

I taught each of my younger brothers and sisters these were naughty words, and told them, "Don't ever let Mama hear you say them." I didn't learn the meaning of some of those words until years later.

I wanted to be like my dad, not a doctor, but grown up. One day he came in from the woods, and found a wood tick embedded in his arm. I watched Mother take the hemostat, and slowly extract the insect. A couple weeks later I was helping, elderly, Anne Spring move some rotting boards to the side of her barn. I was overjoyed when I came home; I had a wood tick just like my daddy.

I asked Bill to tell me about elementary school.

My elementary school had three classrooms, a cafeteria, and restrooms in the basement. Miss Gray taught K-2. She did the best she could with the training she had. It had been many years since she received her schooling. She had a razor strap in the drawer which she took out frequently, and struck the desk near me to get my attention. I don't remember her ever hitting me with it. I enjoyed the swings on the playground, and I loved going higher than the top of the swings; fortunately gravity and fear kept me from going over the top.

Mrs. Lamont was my teacher for grades three thru five. There were about seven kids in my grade. My mother and Mrs. Lamont loaded the entire class in their cars, and we went to the Capitol in

Augusta to see the museum. The kids said the best part of the trip was going to Grandpa Barnes' house on the way home to see their various collections. Grandma gave each of them sea shells from Florida.

Mrs. Twitchell was the best teacher I ever had. She taught grades six thru eight. I often left the house early enough to be in front of her house, so I walked to school with her. Other times, Mike, Daryl, and I met on the schoolhouse steps long before school opened. She unlocked the door, and put us to work cleaning the blackboards and erasers, or gave us extra assignments so we had to use the encyclopedia, etc. We all had great respect for her, and never had any trouble with her.

In the eighth grade several of us had finished all the eighth grade work before Christmas, so she gave us extra assignments.

My biggest memory of hot lunches was the red hotdogs cut into small pieces, and put in a white sauce. I really liked that. We never had red hotdogs at home; I guess they were a Maine food, and Mother was not used to them. In fact, hotdogs were a rare treat for us, because we usually had venison, moose, rabbit, fish, and occasionally chicken. Sometimes I ate the red hotdogs at a bean supper. I loved bean suppers. It was noisy with everybody talking, and all the chairs were filled, and there was a long line waiting for the second seating.

I did not grow much in the seventh and eighth grade. Mother figured if she bought new pants, then I would have a growing spurt. I started high school with only one pair of black trousers, and every night she washed them, and hung them in the shower to dry. Finally, after six weeks she bought another pair of pants. I still did not get much taller.

Hiram did not have a high school; we were bussed fourteen miles away to Fryeburg. When I entered Fryeburg Academy as a freshman it was a whole new world. I knew six kids from Hiram, and there were hundreds at the Academy, many from out of state, and all older and bigger than me. I was a little country boy from a three-room schoolhouse swallowed up by so many strangers.

It was like taking a protected young bull calf that had been kept in a pen his entire life, and suddenly the gate was opened to a whole new world. I found myself in a lot of mischievous type trouble. I spent a lot of time jumping off the bridge into the Saco River until it was too cold. I flatly refused to dress as a girl for freshman's initiation. No way was I going to do that. For my consequences I was given a spoon, and showed a pile of sawdust. I was told I had to retrieve a marble; carry it in the spoon to the other side of the yard, and drop it in a pail. They often heard me say, "No, I am not going to do this," when I thought the initiation request was just too stupid. I found and carried a bucket of marbles.

Pinky True, a teacher and coach, was the one that helped me through my adjustments at Fryeburg. I had received about six years of detentions for minor infractions, and he called me into his office. He said, "You're not very big, and you don't weigh very much, but you're going to join the wrestling team." All detentions were erased except I had to spend one Saturday on clean-up detail. The wresting team gave me a way to vent, and gave me some direction. Coach True was always there for me. The rest of my high school years were spent at Sacopee Valley, the new consolidated high school. I was disappointed they did not have a wrestling program, but I played soccer my sophomore year. I think I played just to say I did it.

We had old junk buses the first couple years after Sacopee opened. The school bus was loaded with the Hiram kids heading for home; we had just crossed the railroad tracks heading up Cornish Station Hill when the bus stalled. Lawrence, the bus driver could not hold the heavy bus with the brakes, and it coasted back down the hill coming to a stop on the railroad tracks. He could not get the bus started, so several of us boys took the matter into our own hands. We departed from the bus, and pushed it backwards off the tracks. Lawrence was in trouble for letting us leave the bus, but he didn't have much choice with a bus full of boys and one adult. Another time Lawrence reprimanded some of us boys, and after he delivered all the kids he went to my house, shaking in his boots, to tell my folks what he had done. He thought they would be fighting mad, but instead they backed him for making us behave.

I never skipped school. Sacopee was too strict. We didn't have a senior skip day.

I went to one prom; Keith Warren drove, and we took the Whitney twins. We ended up marrying them.

I asked, "Do you remember playing the father in the Senior Class play *Our Town?*"

Bill said, "I don't remember that, because the arts were not high on my list of activities."

Buddy tells this story about his brother, Bill.

"One winter day we packed down the snow, with our snowshoes, to make a trail down the mountain. A small pine tree had died from lack of sun light, and it lay across the trail. Billy held up one end of the tree while we slid underneath it. On one trip Steve didn't duck low enough, and his head struck the tree giving him a minor concussion, but not damaging the tree."

We had several dogs through the years. Bill tells about a memorable tragedy when he was quite young.

"Pal, the black cocker spaniel, was hit by a car as it drove around the avenue. She ran to me, I picked her up, and she died in my arms as I carried her into the house. The man kept going, and I was angry. By the time the man drove to the store, he realized he might have struck the dog, he circled around, and pulled into the drive. I felt better to know he cared."

When did you learn to shoot a gun?

I had a shot gun by the time I was ten years old, but I was not allowed to carry it when I checked my trap line, instead I used a stick to club the trapped animals. I had a trap line from the house, and along the ledges to Tuft's field. I trapped several weasels, and one fisher cat. It took me forever to kill him. He was in the trap, and every time I tried to step on the trap to open it he tried to eat my snowshoe. I was not able to get him out the trap. I kept hitting him with a club; when I finally killed him, I took him out of the trap, and put him in my basket back-pack.

When I came home I proudly showed the fisher cat to Dad. I expected praise from him, because I knew Dad hated the vicious predators. Dad yelled, "Oh, my God you have a house cat."

I had no idea what it was; I was only ten years old. When Dad saw I was upset he confessed it was a fisher cat. He said, "Quick get a trash bag, and put the cat in the freezer right now. Don't say anything to anybody, because it is out of season."

The next year when cats were in season, I took the bag out of the freezer, and we called Murray Gilpatrick, the game warden, to come tag it. He measured it, and made out a report. He said, "It's a mighty good looking pelt. If I didn't know better, I'd think this was a February pelt." Everybody just kind of smiled.

When I was about fifteen years old I went rabbit hunting after school. I jumped on the snowmobile with Susie, my beagle, between my legs, and rode out to the hemlock bog near Clarence's. I'd park the snowmobile and let Susie loose. I hunted rabbits for about an hour and one-half.

The fun began when it was time to go home. When Susie chased a rabbit by me, I put the shot gun to my shoulder and shot. Immediately, I ran, and grabbed Susie by the collar, and then I looked to see if I had the rabbit. If I didn't grab her first, she was off chasing another rabbit.

Many times she was left in the woods, because she refused come when I called her, she just kept chasing rabbits. I took off my jacket, and made a nest for her, and went home before I was in trouble. After supper and when my homework was done, I went back for her. I would find her curled up on my coat, and I brought her home.

My first attempt at wheels and speed came when I took apart the old wicker baby buggy. Mother had not used it for a couple years, so I figured it was junk. At age seven, I detached the basket from the frame, and found some boards to lay across the axles for a seat. I hauled the chasse uphill to the top of the driveway, climbed on the seat, pulled my feet off the ground, placed them on the front axle, and whee-e-e-e down the drive I flew. That was exciting, so I pulled it back up the drive for another ride. I was lucky there was not much traffic around the avenue, because each trip took me across the road, and into the neighbor's yard. I also used the chasse to haul wood.

My first go-cart was made out if plywood. I sent to Sears and Roebuck for four wheels. I used a 2x4 for the front axle with a pivot point in the middle, and I used lag bolts to attach the wheels to the axle. I steered it with ropes. It was like a soapbox derby car.

Carl helped his son, Dennis, make a go cart. We dragged them up the mountain to the park, climbed in, and flew down the mountain, and around the tree in the pathway. Away we went to the bottom, and we tried to get them stopped before we came to the railroad tracks. That was the only hill steep enough to get an exciting ride. A wonder we weren't killed.

I rode my bike, and later my go-cart in the road past the patients' parked cars so everyone noticed what a brave daredevil I was. It was a wonder we weren't maimed when Denise, and I raced our bikes during office hours.

Carl brought home a store-bought go-cart for Dennis, so I decided to build one for myself. Bunk had taught me how to weld, and I used some three-quarter inch galvanized water pipe that we tore out of the old hotel before it was dismantled. Galvanized metal is difficult to weld; you can't get a strong weld.

I bought an old Cushman scooter from Bob Widemeyer and tore it apart. I used these wheels for the back wheels of my new cart, and tore apart my previous go-cart for the front wheels. I attached the motor from the Cushman mini bike, and affixed a seat.

After riding this cart for a while the welds started to let go; I tried to reinforce them by welding on some metal bars, but it finally broke in two.

I found some one-inch black, steel pipe, and I commenced building a whole new cart. This time I decided I was going to build a suspension for the front axle. I found an old motorcycle in a junk pile, and took off the rear shocks. I built an A frame shock tower. Now, I had suspension on the front of my go-cart. I used the same Cushman motor and wheels for the rear. This time I bought pneumatic wheels for the front. (They had air in them instead of the hard rubber).

Dennis and I made a racetrack in the field across from the house. We went around in circles until the grass was all hammered down.

I coaxed Buddy to tell me some stories about Billy when they were younger.

I remember Billy was quite a bit older and he spent a lot of time at the village garage where Bunk taught him how to weld. Billy needed more steel for one of his projects. He knew where some old telephone poles were piled on the ground across from the Lyons' house on old 113 near the end of the train trestle. The old telephone poles still had the cross braces on them. He took a crescent wrench over there, and unbolted the braces.

He asked John and me take our bikes across the train trestle. This was when they were still running the train, and I asked, "What do we do if the train comes?"

He answered, "Don't worry about your bikes, just get down here, and jump in the river."

We wheeled our bikes across the trestle, and tied three pieces of steel on each side of our bicycle with binder twine. That was all we could haul, because they were so heavy. Now, we had to wheel them back across the trestle.

Billy had another project a couple years later, and he needed some more steel. They had shut down the old hotel where Hunk Ward lived; Carl Harmon bought it, and planned on demolishing it. We used to play army in there. It had old steel pipes before copper, and we went all over that basement cutting pipes with a hack saw, and sneaking them over to Bunk's garage.

Some of my first jobs were shoveling snow, mowing lawns, and working at the chicken farm close to our house when I was eight years old. I gathered, cleaned, and packed the eggs; he let me bring the cracked eggs home to Mother. I don't remember what I was paid, but he gave me his wool softball uniform from when he was a little boy.

I swam like a fish since a tiny child, and received my junior lifesaving certificate when I was twelve. That summer I went with the Hammond boys to Perley Pond on the Folly Road in North Sebago. There was an old saw mill, and a bunch of sunken logs in the pond. I jumped out of the boat, and dove underwater to tie a rope around a log. They hauled me back into the boat, started the motor, and tug, tug, tug, eventually the logs broke loose, and we dragged them to the shore. We probably reclaimed three truckloads of logs which they sold. I don't remember getting any money, but it was a lot of fun, because I was learning, and spending time with these older boys.

Billy heard about a job at the Fryeburg Nursery when he was thirteen years old. He worked weekends, and all of spring vacation. They took the workers on a tractor drawn wagon to the field where they pulled up seedlings, twenty-five to a bundle. We took him to work Sunday mornings when we were on our way to Upton, and he hitchhiked home in the afternoon. The first time he had difficulty getting a ride home, because he was covered with mud. From then on he took his gym bag, clean clothes, and a book. After working all day he changed to the clean clothes, put the muddy clothes in his gym bag, and carried his book. He got a ride quickly.

What were some of your other jobs?

My next job was working at Camp Blazing Trail, the YWCA camp for girls from Boston. I slept in the tiny log bunk-house. This was before dishwashers of the mechanical type. I was the dishwasher, with my arms in the hot soapy water I scrubbed the dishes, dipped them in boiling water, and set them to air-dry. The kitchen was small, so I carried the large pots and pans outside, and set up my dishwashing station. The girls teased me as they passed by, and with great delight I sprayed them with cold water by placing my thumb over the opening of the hose. When they squealed my heart beat faster.

I worked there two years; the second year John worked with me. He worked at the senior camp, and I was at the junior camp. Percy, the care-taker and family friend, blazed a trail, through the woods, between the two camps. Every day when my work was done I found my way through the woods on this trail to help John, and then we had free time for a couple hours.

We worked seven days a week for two months. Occasionally, I saw Mom when she exchanged my dirty clothes with clean ones, or my dad when he was called to check on a sick camper. I felt all grown-up when I went to the Laundromat in the next town with the councilors.

I want to insert a story here.

Many years later, Dad was taken to the Maine Medical Center, and as the elevator doors opened on the cardiac floor the head nurse met us. In a voice loud enough for all to hear, she said, "Doctor Barnes? Tell your sons not to put my panties in the freezer!" We had no idea what she was talking about. She explained, "I was a nurse at Camp Blazing Trail and your mischievous sons took delight in taking my damp panties from the clothesline and putting them in the freezer, or running them up the flagpole.

Next, I worked for Carl Harmon as a grunt, getting whatever the crew needed. I worked on his crew putting up foundations in North Conway. Transportation was a problem; I needed wheels, so I paid fifty dollars for a broken down inoperable 1963 Harley 250 Sprint motorcycle. I finally had it running after hours of tinkering, but the charging system never did work. I charged it all night long, and then drove to North Conway taking my little battery charger with me. I plugged it in to recharge it all day, ready for the drive home. I had to be home before dark, because the headlights did not work. I never figured out how to fix the electrical system, but I rode that bike a lot.

I worked for Carl for several summers doing construction and foundation work, and then he hired me to maintain all of his cars and trucks. I changed the oil and oil filters on time when they needed it, greased the moving parts, and any other maintenance needed. I was in my glory.

The parents of one of my classmates loved the races at the speedway, and often took me with them. I idolized these racers. I was devastated when Russ Nutting was hurt badly in a car accident. The excitement of the race cars lead me to my next job working at Reynolds Sport Center in his little shop before he built his new one. That summer I worked with Pete Peterson on his race car. The previous winter his brother Donnie was killed in a stupid automobile accident. They were coming home from the races. He and another racer were drag racing on the street; he crashed, and was killed. When I was older I worked on Donnie Stevenson's race car. I was in my glory around these men, and working on their cars. I never wanted to do anything other than tinker with motors, and get greasy.

In the fall of 1970, after I finished my work, I went for a motorcycle ride around the shop. The grass was wet; I missed a turn, crashed, and broke my collar bone badly. They carted me off in an ambulance, and the doctor had to insert a pin to hold the bones together.

Many years later I was surprised that my folks knew Russ Nuttting. Wow, they were friends, and he was in my house.

What made you interested in motorcycles?

My first enthusiasm was when Grandpa Freese took me to Akron on his big Harley, when I was only eight years old, to buy me a Harley cap. I wanted to be just like him. Bunk and Danny, men I looked up to, also had motorcycles. We had a Tote-Goat that I rode a lot in Upton. It was my first two-wheeled machine.

Bill tells:

Lloyd lived next door, and he was a great friend. He worked for the railroad and he told me stories as I hung around him after work while he was doing outdoor jobs. As a special treat, he took me on the very last train ride that went past our house. We drove to Steep Falls, and boarded the train to ride to Hiram.

I was twelve years old, and I sold enough magazine subscriptions for the school to get an electron microscope. I had it set up with bugs and hair, and I wanted my neighbor, Lloyd, to come see all of these things. He had finished cutting wood with his old steam engine saw, had shut it down, and was piling the wood in the barn.

I am standing next to the saw waiting for him to finish. I had my hand on the fly wheel kind of rocking it back and forth. I pulled it up, and it fired, and yanked my hand right down to where the water box was next to the fly wheel. There was a sharp piece of metal, and it skinned off the top of my hand. I was not cut with the saw blade.

I grabbed my hand and ran from Lloyd's to the house. He didn't know what happened. The first sign of blood was on the porch steps. I went into the surgical office with my mother, and when she lifted my hand off the cut blood squirted about ten inches straight up. This was the only time I ever saw my mother queasy in my entire life. She had to leave the room for a minute. I threw a towel back on my hand. There was a whole flap of skin laid back exposing the tendons and veins. I cut a blood vessel, knocked off the cap to my knuckle, and cut down through a tendon that went to my middle finger. Mother put a huge bandage on my hand, and took me to the hospital in Portland.

Hunting season started about two weeks later. I really wanted to go up country hunting. When I came home from school on Friday, Mother changed my bandage, and splinted my middle finger with tongue blades, and we drove to Upton ready to go hunting the next day.

Early in the morning we drove about fifty miles. Dad took off in one direction in the woods. Pete and I walked up a trail until we came to an outcropping of ledges that came around in a quarter-circle. Pete said, "Find a place where you can sit and see, because they run around the bottom of these ledges." I had the old heavy 303 Savage. It was dated 1898, and did not shoot straight for more than 50 feet because the barrel was so pitted, and the bullets almost came out sideways. It had a hinged sight, but it did not have a lock on it. None of this was a factor in my shot, because I don't remember seeing the sights, All I know is I was sitting there, and I heard the chunk, chunk up the trail right where we walked. We were only a hundred yards in the woods. I am getting madder than hell because someone is coming up from where we parked the jeep when all of a sudden I saw two deer right in front of me. I was surprised when I hit one of them, and so excited. It was quite a feat for a twelve year old. After the excitement died down I realized the tongue blades had broken and jabbed into my hand. Pete helped me dress out the deer because he didn't want me to get deer blood in my wound.

Tell me some stories about your college years.

    I spent two years studying auto mechanics and loved it. About this time I had an accident with your car and you said, "You can never drive my car again." I saw an ad in the newspaper for a one owner 1955 red Mustang. I paid $500.00 it. I was excited; I had a car of my own! I sanded it down, fixed all the dings, and painted it myself. I searched for the brightest yellow I could find, and located Ford Competition Yellow. It was a color that had not been used yet. It didn't come out on a mustang until late 1969.

    The Vietnam war was in full swing. You took me to Lester Hammond's house to register for the draft; I had an S-1 college deferment. The government was not getting enough volunteers, so they set up a lottery. They drew out 365 balls, and attached that number to your file. If you were number one, you didn't wait for the letter, you just showed up at the recruitment office.

    I remember a group of us at college were going to listen to the lottery drawing together. They were constructing a new building on campus. The steel structure was up, and the floors were laid, but there were no walls. Somehow we climbed to the top of the structure taking an old portable radio, a few bottles of 3.2 beer, and we sat on the edge of this building three floors up listening to the drawing. I ended up being number 305. I will never forget that number as long as I live.

    College kids can be quite resourceful. There was a boy at college who put himself through school with his forgery business. The drinking age was twenty at that time.

    Somehow he obtained a blank draft card, and photocopied both sides, and then he filled it out. He glued the two sides together and then laminated it, roughed it up, and made it dirty. I am sure it would not pass close scrutiny, but it was good enough to get a 3.2 beer at the little corner store. He charged $3.00 apiece.

Air Force

I decided I was not going to work at the pallet mill in Steep Falls the rest of my life. There was nothing for me in Maine. I was an angry young man, angry at the world. I was walking down the street in Portland, and saw a recruiting office; I walked in, talked with the recruiter, and signed up. I knew I wanted to do something mechanical, and I did not want to end up being a chef. At that time they had a guaranteed career field, so I knew I was going to end up being a crew chief. I went in July 13, 1976. That was the scariest day of my life.

I was twenty-four-years-old when I enlisted in the air force, and I had a sense of responsibility most of the younger men did not have. I took my job very seriously. After my first duty station in Georgia, I made crew chief for the entire base within a month, and a lot of people who had more time than me were not very happy. They were thinking, here comes this young guy with only ten months training, and he has out-performed all of us. This created friction with some of the men.

Many of the pilots wanted me to be their crew chief. They talked with the OPS (operation planning staff) officer, and requested me to be appointed to their aircraft, because my five planes were always the best shooting aircraft, the best bombing aircraft, and the best maintained aircraft out of the fifty-six aircraft we had on the base. It wasn't because I was any better, but because I knew everything about that plane; I knew what it liked, and what it did not like.

I learned this by debriefing the pilots each time they came back from a run. This wasn't my job requirement, but I asked each pilot, and then I passed on this information. If it bombed short I told the pilot to compensate for it, if it shot to the left, I informed the pilot. Soon they trusted me, and they had bull's-eye scores.

One of the perks for making crew chief was getting a free ride in an F-4 jet. I was some excited to think I was going to get one hour in the sky in a fighter. Joe, my pilot wanted to take me in the worse way. He had over two hundred missions in Vietnam. He was going to take me to the Jacksonville Air Station in Florida, and do a low-run fly-by over the run way.

The commander became aware of this and he said, "No. This is a bad situation and you're not doing it." They assigned me a pilot from another fighter squadron. We were flying along and he said, "Do you see the interstate?"

My brain interpreted, "Do you see the speedway?" and I said, "No, I don't see it."

We were flying at 6,000 feet, and he said, "Look straight overhead into the canopy," and he flipped the plane upside down and asked, "What do you see?"

"I see a highway."

"Yeah, that's it." He flipped it back over, and we headed for the bombing range. The pilots were not allowed to beak the sound barrier, which is mock speed, over land. So, he went to .9 mock at 10,000 feet. Because this flight was rushed they did not have time to put me into the altitude chamber, so they restricted me to a 17,000 foot ceiling. The pilot went into a 4-G climb, and started spiraling. The way I knew he was spiraling was, because there was an optical light which is a ball with an artificial horizon, and it was spinning. I saw the sun go by every-so-often. He started pitching it out at 17,000 feet, and went over the top at 22,000 feet. We were going almost 100 miles per hour. He pitched it in at about a G and one-half negative dive, and at 17,000 feet he pulled it up flat and level. At this time I was swallowing so I didn't lose it. All of this took only six and one-half seconds. I started having difficulty breathing, so I went to 100 per cent oxygen. I was breathing deeply, and I started getting nauseated.

He said, "Take the stick." He knew he had to distract me. "Turn to this heading and fly level."

I said, "I can't maintain the altitude."

"What are those things on your left side?"

"Those are the throttles."

"Well, that is what they are for. If you can't keep the altitude, use the throttles."

"All right, here we go! You didn't tell me I could play with those. What are these switches that say bomb racks, can I play with them too?" Of course, there were no weapons on board at that time. After almost an hour I flew back to the base, and lined up the plane for the approach, and he took back the controls.

That was quite an hour. It taught me to respect what those guys went through. What we did was nothing; we went only about 4 G's at max. These pilots come back from combat training, and I went inside and saw 6 ½ or 7 Gs and 3 Gs negative recorded. The inside of the cockpit was covered in frost where they had the air conditioning set so low, and yet their clothes were drenched with sweat.

Because of my connections with Joe, one of my pilots, he snuck me into the flight simulator where I learned how to do engine starts, and stuff like that.

Here I am barely a two striper Airman First Class. This is stuff Buck Sergeants are just starting to learn. Even though I was able do this I didn't have enough rank to do it legally as an Airman First Class. I was not able to get orders until I made senior airman. They had to sneak me in through the back door to do the flight simulator stuff.

Woody and I went through tech school at the same base, and we were the only two in the entire ninth Air force that had licenses to generate the aircraft. They had to be run every day.

Either a weapons officer, or commander had to be with me. I had the choice of the front seat, or back seat to do the high speed taxi checks. I would taxi right to the point of wheels-up. I was able to do this only on Saturdays or Sundays. I checked with control to see if they had any planes scheduled for high speed taxi checks. Then they had to find a pilot willing to come in on the weekend to ride with me. If they found one, I went to my boss and said, "I'll volunteer for duty this weekend if I can get two days off next week, and then I let the OPS Officer know I had weekend duty. We drag raced jets up and down the runways. You had to learn how to play their game. Eventually, I became very good at playing their game. I was very proud of my time there, and the things I learned. I took it very seriously.

Saving the Plane

Bill describes what happened on this particular night.

Toward the end of my duty, I was with what they called Red Flag. It was a live-fire scenario which they did in Las Vegas. They brought in planes from different bases and other countries. They did this live fire training with real bombs and real bullets. I went once, but this year I didn't go, because I was too close to being discharged. I chose to stay behind with three aircraft that didn't go. I was the only one on second shift. They flew each airplane once a day, F-4's had to be flown; the more they flew the better they operated. If they sat they broke. We took each aircraft out for a one hour mission every day. My job was to check each plane, and make sure every plane was ready and fueled, and then I could go home. Sometimes I was finished by seven, and other times I had to stay the whole shift.

It was just before dusk, and I was going over the last aircraft, checking the list. I was up on the back bone of the aircraft, closing the canopy for the night. I flipped the button to close the canopy down, and as I stood up I saw sparks out on the tarmac. It was like the Fourth of July.

There were three planes on the tarmac, part of the 339th squadron, and I saw some guys over there working. I am assigned to the 70th squadron. The 339th flew just regular training missions at the base. All of a sudden I saw the cockpit explode, and sparks flew. What happened is the sparks ignited the residual fuel on the tarmac from the overflow fuel hoses (bowsers) on the wing tanks. The fire followed up the hoses and into the wings, and then the entire aircraft was engulfed in flames.

As soon as I saw the initial sparks and fire, I grabbed my radio and immediately called control, "May-day, may-day, Able 1. Aircraft fire."

I jumped down and into a Coleman, a tow vehicle, which had a tow bar hooked on the back of it. It was parked next to the aircraft I was on. I immediately swung around heading toward the fire. Two- guys from the repair shop were walking by, and I commandeered them.

I shouted, "You're with me; we have to tow these aircraft!" I immediately went to the aircraft next to the burning plane; the fire department was not there yet. The fire department was closer to the fire than I was. By now the aircraft was at least 30% engulfed in flames. I backed up, and the men hooked the tow-bar onto the front wheels. It was on a downhill ramp, and the aircraft was leaning into the wheel-stops. They were unable to remove the wheel stops. I looked back over my shoulder at the burning aircraft, and I was looking right up the barrel of a 30 millimeter loaded gun. I thought this isn't good, because if the fire gets into that chamber, I am dead.

I yelled for the men to get away. I gunned the Coleman, and yanked the plane out of the stops. It ripped the nose out of the aircraft, ripped out all the seals, and I crossed the secure-area line, which we are not supposed to do.

There was a cop there and he tried to stop me. He pointed his gun at me, but I knew he had no bullets, because they were not allowed to have a loaded gun on base. I swung around, and took off down the runway looking for a place to park the aircraft. The fire truck was coming toward me, and they swung around, and into the area I had just vacated. They started putting foam onto the fire.

I dropped the air plane off, and went back to get the second plane out of there. At this point the burning aircraft blows up, and the fire truck catches on fire.

Now, there wasn't much the firemen could do. We are talking 3,000 gallons of jet fuel in the plane. They saw the flames eight miles away in the town of Valdosta. I not only saw them, thirty yards away, but I felt them. I was able to tow the second aircraft, and parked it next to the first.

Immediately, I went back to the flight shack while they are still trying to work on the fire. I had enough presence of mind to sit down, and write down everything that had happened, exactly the way it happened while it was all fresh in my mind. I put it in an envelope, sealed it, and I put it in my NCOIC's (Non commission officer in charge, my boss) office. At this point, I think the Sky Cop had given up on me. I don't remember seeing him again after I left. By now it is eleven o'clock, and I had to get home to be with the girl's, because Maureen had to leave for work on the night shift.

My boss did not go to Red Flag. He was the highest officer in my squadron on base. I am at home, and I get a call about five o'clock in the morning. "Hey Bill, get in here!"

"I can't, I have the kids."

"Don't take time to dress them, just wrap them up in a blanket, and I will meet you at the main gate. My wife will be there to take care of them."

I said, "Is it that bad?"

"Worse."

I think, oh shit now what is going on?

I get to the base and go over the whole thing with him. Come to find out the men of the 339th squadron were all in the shop playing cards. They didn't know any of this had happened until the fire truck went by. They looked out the window, and saw one of their aircraft burning.

They were filing charges against me for everything from illegal towing procedures to anything they could think of to cover their asses. I was going to have Court Marshall Charges brought against me. After I finished explaining it to my boss I then had to go to Major Hurley, the officer in charge of the entire base. Major Hurley had also been a pilot in Vietnam, and he was also one of the pilots on the list trying to get me to be the crew chief for his aircraft. He was a good friend of Joe's and a friend of mine. If we met off base we were on a first name basis.

By the time they investigated the whole thing, it was turned around and the 339th was in whole ton of crap, and I received the highest medal a noncommissioned officer can receive in peace time.

It was presented to me in front a great reception of people, my wife, my kids, my dog, and the postman, because I received it in the mail twenty months after I was discharged from the air force.

This Airman's Medal was not in my permanent record, because I had been discharged. I had to go to the Veterans Administration to have them put it in my file.

Running

While I was in the Air Force, Joe Fuller, a close friend, and I started running; our Air Society group (like an ROTC group) were putting on a race to raise money. We agreed to run to help them out. We trained two miles a day for two weeks to run a six mile race. After that I had the bug for it, and I started running longer distances. I ran faster and faster and decided I wanted to run the New York Marathon. I was running fifty to eighty miles a week. My goal was to do the race in three and one-half hours. I did a fourteen mile run every Saturday, running through two towns and down the narrow gauge railroad path. I loved that, it was a mind clearing experience. Two weeks before the marathon I ran twenty miles from Derry to Nashua and back; the only time I ran twenty miles.

The day of the marathon was chilly. We boarded a bus, and they took us over the Verrazano Bridge where the race started. They had the seeded runners in front, and then a rope and the runners were supposed to line up roughly according to their time behind the rope. I got as close to that rope as I could, even though I should have been back another hundred yards. That was my competitive nature.

I had a back pack with my name on it. I stripped down to what I was going to wear: shirt, shorts, and shoes. I put my warm up clothes in my back pack, and throw it on the bus. They took it back and packed everything in a big tent. When the race was over I went back, and picked up my stuff. Maurine and the girls would be waiting at the finish line approximately when I expected to cross.

I took off running with the pack, and I felt really comfortable. At the five mile marker I was way too fast. I was on a 3 hour 5 minute pace, but it felt good. I got through mile thirteen and am still on the same pace. I passed fifteen and I am still good. Maybe I can do this I thought. I tried to stay comfortable. When I got to mile twenty-one it was like a baseball bat him me between the eyes. It was pure torture, and I was forced to slow down.

I crossed the line in 3 hours 29 minutes and 20 seconds. The pain was unending, I walked, I crawled, and I stood bent over. That was the end of my marathon days.

Job

I had ninety days paid leave when I was discharged, and I planned on doing nothing during that time. I had been home a couple weeks when I saw an ad in the newspaper, "OPEN HOUSE! FREE COFFEE AND DONUTS."

The next morning I jumped in the car and went for my free breakfast, a cup of coffee and a few dozen donuts. I filled out the employment application, a prerequisite to getting the donuts.

When my belly was full I took a tour of the plant. I didn't think I would be hired into this one hundred million dollar facility. They told me the person I needed to talk with wasn't there. When he gets back, we'll call you and set up another appointment. It sounded like the royal blow off to me.

Before I got home there was a phone call, and they wanted me back there the next morning. They told me they were looking for a maintenance tech. I met with another supervisor, and they dismissed me. By the time I got home they had called, and made a job offer. I called them back and took the offer. I was back to work three weeks after I got out of the Air Force.

What they didn't tell me was the room they put me in was used for photolithography. They told me the last tech quit last week, and I was going to have to teach myself how this room works. The process involved pneumatic, hydraulic, and electronic operations. When the girls were processing, I lay on my back under the six million dollar machine, and watched everything that was happening. I taught myself how the machine worked or how it thinks. I had to read a lot about Photolithography.- They print circuits onto silicone.

I figured out how to set up preventive maintenance, and within a year, two of the manufactures made me job offers to work for them in field service.

I was one of the last people to have the guaranteed 45 month GI Bill. The company paid my tuition as long as I maintained a B average. I worked during the day, and took two classes at night. The GI Bill gave me $500 a month for the next four years.

I received my associate degree in digital electronics from Hesser College, and then I went to a New Hampshire college taking business classes.

This company had a lot of runners, and I became involved with a corporate team. At lunch hour we ran seven miles. I started working more on speed training and less on endurance.

After that I was into racquetball. There was a court near where I lived. I cut my eye lid open, and they wanted me to forfeit the tournament. I asked for a fifteen minute time out; I cut two butterflies and taped the gash closed. I went back, and won the match. The butterflies held so well I never saw a doctor.

Log Homes

I built my first prefabbed log home after looking at several different kits. I settled on Lincoln Logs.

I bought the kit from a dealer in New Hampshire. They gave me four hours on-site instruction when it was delivered. Buddy came over and helped me. The dealer came down to look at it, and he liked what I was doing. He asked me if I was interested in doing another house in the next town. I did that one plus my job. Construction got to be a lot more fun than my job, so I gave my notice and quit.

Soon I signed on as a dealer and builder. My company grew, and at one time I had thirty employees. It was always a problem finding good workers. As a contractor I did the wiring, plumbing, and installing the heating systems. I was self-taught in all these fields.

One of the things extremely frustrating to me growing up was how if anything was damaged, I was the first one to be blamed whether it was my fault or not. For example the old yellow Ski-doo the throttle froze, and when I pulled into the garage, it wouldn't stop, and it broke the cowling. And yet Joh and I were in Bailey's field playing tag on the snowmobiles at night without the headlights on, and he drives it into a four inch tree and up about thirteen feet, and put a big dent in the front of the motor ski. The only comment was, "Are you okay?"

John

John, the self-assured independent young man, was my second child. This long, slender baby was crawling at a very young age. He did not get up on his hands and knees, but with his arms bent in front of him he pulled himself across the floor with his legs dragging behind. This scrawny adventurer turned his head sideways, and pulled himself under a bureau. I could not find him until I heard the squealing of frustration as his head was too large to back out without turning it.

John was nicknamed "Punky" when he was five months old, because we found him hiding behind a chair in the living room shoveling pumpkin pie into his mouth as fast as he could. No one ever confessed giving him that piece of pie. Billy would not tell. He was called "Punky" until he entered school, and then I insisted he should be called John.

He did not like being reprimanded, and when scolded he changed the subject by looking out the window and saying, "See cow." At eight months while sitting in his highchair he looked out the window, and saw his first falling snow and exclaimed, "Noose." To this day the family refers to the first snow of the winter as *noose*.

As a baby John's head was covered with gentle curls. When people started thinking he was a girl I decided it was time for a haircut. Trying to get a seven month old to hold still was a monumental task, so I put an extra sheet on his crib, and after he fell asleep I started using the scissors and clippers. He woke up when I tried to turn his head to clip the other side. With toys as a diversion, I finally finished the job, and then took away the extra sheet and hair clippings. He never sat in a barber's chair the rest of his life.

River

I remember the day I took two-year-old John for a walk across the bridge to the post office. On the way home we paused, so he could throw small stones into the river. That was a big mistake. Monday, while I was doing the laundry, John escaped out the door, and headed for the river. I heard him crying as Stubby was holding his hand, and walking him home. I made sure the gate was closed and locked to their play yard. As soon as I turned my back he squirmed under the fence, and was headed for the river. As Stubby was bringing him home again I told him, "You should warm his bottom."

He said, "Oh, I couldn't do that." Pretty soon I heard John screaming as Stubby was once again bringing him home, switching at his shoe tops with a dried golden rod. John never left the yard again.

Childhood

Every kid loves a birthday party, and every kid wants to be invited, but this party ended in disaster and animosity. There was near hated toward the parents of the birthday boy. Eight little boys age six to eight trudged through the snow on this cold February day. Games were played, presents opened, cake and hot cocoa served, and all were happy. The mother announced there was one more game to be played before the party was over. Everybody was a winner in this game; each little boy was handed a large grocery bag stapled shut containing a live bunny rabbit. They were told not to open the bag until they were home.

Each household had a similar reaction; where can we keep the rabbit in this cold weather? That night the bunnies were housed in large corrugated boxes. Fathers were not too happy having to give up their free time to build a hutch. Some hardly knew how to use a hammer. The next morning pure white Snowball was not to be found, instead a drab gray bunny emerged from the warm ashes of the fireplace where he had found warmth. Pepper was still camouflaged in the ashes.

The annual school program was rapidly approaching and John's second grade was going to skip across the stage to cowboy music. Big problem, John did not know how to skip. I spent many afternoons on the front porch in view of all the neighbors trying to teach him, but nothing worked. Finally, I wrote down what each leg was to do in sequence on a note pad, and approached this like a mathematical problem. I called out, and performed the first four movements, and then had John do them with me repeatedly. Next I added the next four actions, and repeated them several times, and as he grasped this we moved on until he mastered this new skill.

Many Saturday mornings a young boy that lived almost a mile away showed up at our door to join my children in watching television cartoons. My kids did not like me to say, "Okay, it is time for you to go home." I finally figured out the diplomatic way of getting rid of this kid. I announced, "Okay, turn off television, and get out the books; it's time to study." All moaned, and grumbled in unison as Martin headed for the door. We watched him trudge to the neighbor's house to continue watching his favorite programs.

John was not one to complain, he just quietly took care of the problem. One of the dogs threw up on the kitchen floor, and the baby sitter could not clean up the mess, so John stepped forward, and took care of the problem.

John, at a very young age, had the ability to unwrap a Christmas gift and then rewrap it with nobody the wiser. I was suspicious that one of the kids was doing this, but did not know which one. I swapped the names and gender of the gifts and taped this secret code to the bottom of my jewelry box. I wrapped the presents as soon as I came home from shopping. One afternoon John came into the kitchen; his face was red, the veins in his neck were enlarged, and he was breathing fire like a dragon. The flaming words came from his mouth, "I hate pink" A-ha, I knew who the night invader was, because Diane's pink sweater held John's name.

The boys didn't care if their shirt-tails were tucked into their pants. There was a simple solution. I sewed pink lace on their shirt-tails.

There was a two-cent deposit on all soda bottles. One morning John started down the River Road in search of cast off bottles. He put two bottles in his bag, and then he spotted a windblown one-dollar bill wrapped around the stem of a weed. He leaped off his bicycle to retrieve it. Excitement soared through his veins as he pedaled home to brag about his find.

Pony

We owned a twenty acre field of wild blueberries on a mountain top in Upton. All the children earned money picking, and selling the berries. John was probably the most dedicated picker of all the children. By the time he was ten years old he could pick more blueberries than he could sell to his local customers. He convinced his dad to take him to Sebago where he sat up his stand in front of Jordan's Store using several milk crates. He watched the people as they walked by, and deduced they probably were too lazy to bake, so he asked me to bake some blueberry muffins. I negotiated with him, and said I would make the muffins, but he had to wash all the baking dishes. His profits increased.

He had been saving his money in hopes of buying a pony. He approached the local owner of several ponies. He pointed to the far corner of the pasture and asked, "How much is that white pony?"

The farmer said, "$375.00."

John was disappointed and yet determined. He asked, "How much is that spotted pony?"

The reply was, "$300.00."

John only had $90.00. He asked again, "How much is the brown pony?"

His whole body ached as he heard the reply, "$250.00."

He was about to walk away when the man asked him how much money he had. The man said enthusiastically, "I may have just what you need as he lead him to the barn, and showed him a shiny chrome buggy. He said, "It is only $75.00."

John said not a word, but walked to the car, and got inside. His dejected look prompted me to ask, "What is wrong?"

He answered strongly, "I don't know what kind of dummy that man thinks I am. That buggy is no good to me without a pony."

John continued to pick berries and save his money, but he never got his pony.

On Sundays the fields were loaded with pickers. John was looking for a diversion as he carried his pail filled with the blue orbs to the house. He sat them in the kitchen, and went to the game room; he picked up the bearskin rug from the floor. He traversed out the back door, and through the woods emerging in the lower field on his hands and knees covered with the black, hairy pelt.

He crawled quite a ways before he was detected. He heard a little girl scream, and then others were making sounds of fright. The delight he got from this prank warmed his insides.

One Sunday Dad forgot to take his medicine. I sent Scotte age four, and her older brother John age nine to deliver the medicine. I told them, "He is in the woods using his chain saw." The two of them left on an adventure of great importance. Little did they know what an adventure it was going to be.

About two hours later, Dad appeared at the house. I asked, "Did John give you your medicine?"

"No I haven't seen him. I've been cutting down some dead trees," he replied. "Why did you ask?"

"I gave him your medicine and told him to take it to you."

I worry they might be lost. We've got to start looking for them. "Billy, listen to me carefully. I want you to stand right here on the porch, and keep blowing this horn. Always point it in the same direction. That will help John follow the sound." The horn was four feet tall and the bell was over twelve inches across. It had been used on Lake Umbagog to guide ships in the fog.

I started through the woods, and quickly realized I was going to be lost too. I went back to the field, and asked Dad to go looking for them, and I would stay on the Mollidgewak Trail. I promised I would not leave the trail.

John and Scotte entered the woods going down the Mollidgewak Trail. They had gone quite a ways when they heard the chain saw, and they headed for it. It was a long hike. Finally, the sound of the saw was close. A man looked up, and shut off his saw. John asked, "Have you seen Doctor Barnes?"

The man said, "No. Are you kids lost?"

"No, but can you tell us where we are?"

"You are in New Hampshire," the man offered.

John thanked him and turned back the way they had come. He knew what general direction he had to go. Scotte was pulling at his shirt and sobbing, "We are lost. Why did you tell him we weren't?" They came to a pile of wood that John remembered seeing before. Just then he noticed a bear print, which he had not notice before.

He asked Scotte what she would do if they came upon a bear. He told her running wouldn't work. "Do you think you could climb that pile of wood?" They were both getting tired. John thought he heard something. They listened intently, and decided it sounded like a horn. He said, "Maybe Mother is blowing the horn to guide us. I think we are getting closer." They continued their walk, and stopped frequently to listen for the horn. John knew he was right, and they continued forward. Suddenly, they heard something different. John said, "I think it is a moose. Come hide with me behind this rock. "Shhh, don't worry, I'll protect you." John took a peek around the rock, and he was really surprised. His eyes could hardly believe the moose was his mother.

Jobs

John's next money making project was selling Amway products. He carried with him a clear peanut butter jar the size of a fish bowl. He asked the lady of the house to fill it thee-fourth full with cold water, and to bring him some clean washcloths. He put one teaspoon of S-A-8 into the water and immersed the washcloth. He knew this was an extremely strong solution, because it was only two or three tablespoon for a whole washer full of clothes. The lady could see the accumulated soap racing to leave the washcloth. This was impressive. She saw her clean clothes getting cleaner. His sales were limited due to lack of transportation.

His next job was at Camp Blazing Trail washing pots and pans, and bringing items from the pantry for the next meal. Granny, the cook, was delight with the work ethics of this neat young man. They got along just great. His brother, Bill, worked in the adjoining senior camp. He spent eight weeks of his summer there and put most of his money in the bank. Bill moved to another job the next year and Buddy joined John at Blazing Trail.

When the evening program was concluded, the girls returned to their cabins, and climbed into bed before lights-out. John was standing on the knoll next to the flagpole, and when the cabin lights disappeared he reverently played taps.

It was time for John to move on to another job. He worked at Simpson's Beach snack bar for two summers; he started outback preparing foods and running the Fry-o-later. The second year he worked out front on the grill fixing hamburgers and hot dogs. Everyone got to know him. This gave him a chance to associate with other teenagers.

Teens

We had a new hound dog and Dad was training her to chase bobcats. To do this he set a trap to catch a bobcat, so the dog could associate the small with the hunt. One morning he returned to the house after finding a cat in his trap. He wanted the kids to share in the experience. While they were putting on warm winter coats and pants Billy rode his snowmobile up the mountain, and built a fire at the Frenchman's Camp, then came home to ferry each of the younger kids to the top of the mountain. Mom made sandwiches for the outing, and Dad leashed Judy, and held her between his knees as he rode another snowmobile to the trap.

John came to the camp, and told the kids to finish their sandwiches, and he took them to the bobcat. They heard the dog barking long before they spotted the bobcat. The girls were scared, but they were told they could go closer to see the bobcat better. When they got there they could see his blue eyes, and they covered their ears, because the dog was barking so loudly. Everyone was excited and having fun. Judy grabbed ahold of the bobcat, and bit his tail; the bobcat fought back. The cat grabbed Judy on the back and scratched her face. Judy barked, and she fought back. The bobcat started toward the girls, and Daddy yelled to get out of the way. The girls grabbed sticks, so they could hit the bobcat if he got too close. Buddy stepped in front of the girls, and spread out his arms to protect them. Scotte said, "Terry, you better get ready to clobber that thing because he might come toward us anytime now." Pretty soon Dad handed John the 22 rifle, and he shot the bobcat in one ear, and it came out the other ear.

I asked John, "How were you able to shoot him with one shot?"

He answered. "It was easy, because if I missed, Billy got his turn to shoot."

John was quite musical, and he started playing the trumpet at a young age. Mr. Fuchs came to our house to give him lessons, and soon he was playing in the elementary band in Fryeburg. The band played for the Hiram Memorial Day Parade. When the band stopped on the bridge to honor the sailors, Mr. Fuchs asked John to slip away, and go to the end of the bridge to play the echo to Taps. John thought it would be more effective if the crowd could not see the echo, so he crawled down under the bridge. As soon as Taps was finished on the bridge, he pointed his trumpet downstream, and answered with gentle tones from his trumpet. John did this every year until he was killed.

The officers from the American Legion asked John to play at all military funerals.

Every evening the patients in the waiting room were serenaded by John practicing on his horn. As the years went on, the instruments of the other children chimed in with their different songs.

Years later John went to the hardware department at Sears and tapped every saw in the store to see which one gave him the best tone. He played the saw with a felt covered wooden hammer tapping it. He never had a bow to play on the saw.

If you live in Maine, you better learn to enjoy the snow, because there is a lot of it. One year the snow was so deep John walked directly onto the kitchen roof at Upton. John, Diane, and Buddy climbed up onto the main roof about twenty-five feet high. Diane jumped feet first into the drifted snow, and immediately the boys jumped on either side of her packing her in the deep snow. They left her entombed while they pursued other activities. She could not move anything except her vocal cords. Someone had to take a shovel to break her loose in order to push the off button to squelch her wailing.

Burnt Mountain Ski slope opened just five miles from the house. This gave John an opportunity to ski frequently. His skiing rapidly improved. Soon he was on the ski patrol team.

He borrowed his father's short skis and became quite acrobatic. This was before snow boards.

John loved people. When he was a junior in high school he volunteered to be a mentor to a boy in the second grade who had recently moved to Maine. Pete was having difficulty adapting to his new environment. John and Pete were given permission to explore the woods near the school one afternoon. Unfortunately John was killed three days before this event was to take place. This young boy never forgot their few brief encounters before John's death.

A young girl was kidnapped from the local ice skating pond, and there was nothing we could do by the time we were notified. As we returned home our children came running, and said they had a patient in the surgical room. We found a teenage girl sitting there with a cut on her knee, and deep abrasions on her hands. When we asked what happened, John interjected, "She fell jumping out of a car. I was over by the creamery, I saw sparks, and saw her fall. I ran to help her, and the car took off."

I asked, "What do you mean sparks?"

John said, "From her skates. When she jumped, and the skates hit the pavement it caused a spark."

Because John saved the girl from being kidnapped, he didn't get into too much trouble for leaving the house while we were gone.

These are some stories Diane tells:

John had an eight-track player in his car. He was a very careful driver, and sometimes he loaded the car full of us kids, and half of the neighbors to take us swimming. I don't know how he had the patience with all the music, yelling, and so forth, but that was John. He was usually the brains behind a lot of things that happened. Buddy was always looking for the short-cut, but John had to think things through, and make a plan. Whether we were building a snow fort, or chopping down a tree. John had the adult view. John always looked after us girls. One day we had a flat tire, and he made us go stand in the ditch away from the car while he changed the tire. There are other memories like scuba diving. Buddy was more the animal toward us girls, probably because we were closer in age.

John was like a mother hen to us girls. If he thought our skirts were a little too short, or any other problem with our clothes, he made us change before we went to school. If we started to tell a joke at the supper table, we had to whisper it to him for approval. I suppose this kept us from getting into trouble a few times.

Scotte tells, "John was tired of my pestering him to tie my sneakers. He sat me down, and showed me how to tie my own shoes.

Accident

John's slender frame and long legs made him a winner on the track team. His determination made him perfect to run the two-mile event. State law prohibited him from entering any other track event; they felt it would be excessive strain on the growing youth. Friday afternoon, in competition with the school's top rival, the coach and John decided to change John's race from the two-mile run to running the one-mile, relay, and hurdles (which he had never jumped.)

The loud ringing of the telephone awoke us at one o'clock in the morning. "This is Helen; there is an automobile accident in front of my house." We bolted out of bed, dressed in the dark, because there was no electricity. I headed to the office to gather all the emergency bags.

I stood on my tip-toes, and glanced out the window. "My God, it's John." His car was not in the drive. The agonizing drive to the scene of the accident seemed to take forever. The car was not badly damaged, but when we opened the door, his crumpled body was convulsing. Our trained eyes knew this meant he had an injury to his brain, but we did not suspect he would be dead within eighteen hours.

Through the miracle of medicine they were able to harvest his eyes and kidneys to be transplanted into four hoping, prayerful strangers. At that time these were the only organs for which transplantation had been perfected.

Ironically, there was a parade that afternoon in Hiram. The band was there, but there was no echo to the playing of Taps. The evening serenade in the Barnes' household would be missing its key player. The veterans had to scurry to find another for their funerals.

While working with the funeral director the question arose about insurance. He said, "Of course, he won't qualify for the social security death benefit, because he has not worked enough."

I disputed this and asked him to make application, because I felt he had worked enough quarters to qualify. I was right, but what were we going to do with this money, and John's savings account. None of us could touch it. It felt like blood money. We took all of this money plus his ten thousand dollar insurance policy, and established a scholarship at Sacopee High School. Every year for the past forty-three years some deserving student has received this welcomed help in John's memory.

Gail Bell, one of John's summer friends, wrote the following song to the melody of "Candle in the Wind" in John's memory.

John's Song

Seventeen, young, and frail,
But with determination hard as nails,
You sped through life, knowing where to go.
Your feeling that you didn't understand,
Were what ,made you so very grand,
And your kindness just couldn't help but to show.

> *{Chorus}*
> *White clouds were your laughter.*
> *So light, and free, and gay.*
> *Your eyes were like the sunshine,*
> *Of a blue sky on a summer's day.*

People meant a lot to you,
So there wasn't anything you wouldn't do,
To help a soul who couldn't walk alone.
The love that you had for life,
Would help you over any strife.
And you did things without a complaining tone.
> *{Chorus}*

When your life had ceased,
Who would have thought that time would be the least,
Of all the virtues that you had owned?
With all the things you had to give,
Why is it God didn't let you live?
But even gone your love remains and grows.
> *{Chorus}*

Buddy

It was November 30, 1956, the last day of hunting season, and Doc had not tagged a deer. The minute the last patient left the office he changed into his hunting clothes, and was headed for the woods. Just before he closed the door I said, "Don't linger too long at the checking station gabbing with the other hunters, because I am in labor." A look of concerned, questioning, panic came over his face wondering if he dared to leave. I waved him out the door. He returned empty-handed, and was relieved to find me preparing supper, and not standing on my head in the corner to prevent the baby from falling out.

That evening after the boys were in bed we had the neighbor lady, Mrs. Mac, come stay with them. The contractions continued every five minutes, but Doc was in no hurry to leave for the hospital, because he wanted to watch the boxing match on television.

We left for the hospital after the winner's gloved hand was raised. As we neared the hospital, a giant, colorful billboard displaying a luscious steak dinner at Valley's Restaurant caught my eye. I started longing for that luscious meal.

My contractions wanted to stop, and the only way I could keep them going was to pace the creaking, old, wooden floor of the obstetrical wing. It was the second floor in the old house, which was the original hospital.

While I walked a half marathon that night, Doc curled up on a cot in intern quarters and slept.

Finally, I am reclining on the flat, cold, hard delivery table waiting for the doctors to finish scrubbing, and to proceed with the delivery. It seemed to be taking them forever. To pass the time away, I kept talking about the steak dinner at Valleys, and how I would really enjoy it right now. Then, I changed the subject. I wanted to be awake for this delivery, so I said, "I'll knock the block off any nurse that tries to put me asleep."

Doctor Morse replied as he continued to scrub, "Would you like to give yourself the anesthesia?"

I had never heard of such a thing. They placed a cylinder, similar to a flashlight, in my hand. Attached to one end of it was a mask I could hold over my nose and mouth. When I had my next contraction Doctor Morse said, "Put the mask over your nose, and take a deep breath." At the next contraction he said, "Take another deep breath."

This was great, it eased the discomfort, and I was in control. I took another breath when instructed. My next recollection was hearing my husband shouting, "Breath you darn fool; it's oxygen!"

Apparently the third breath knocked me out. After the delivery a nurse placed an oxygen mask on my face; I was holding my breath not wanting to fall asleep.

An hour later I was tucked snuggly into my bed when there was a knock at the door, and a hospital employee entered carrying a tray. I was curious; I lifted the cover. There was my complete steak dinner at ten o'clock in the morning.

Buddy was a happy baby, and was quickly nicknamed *Grinny Bear*. He had big blue eyes, and a constant grin which he carries to this day.

A vision his parents fondly remembered was watching four-month-old Buddy in his crib, lying on his stomach, with his head tilted back and to the side. He had his hand on the bottom of the bottle holding it upside down in his mouth while drinking it dry.

As a newborn baby his hair stood on end, and at about four months of age it was longer, and started to lie down. The solution was to give him a butch haircut. He wore a butch haircut until high school when the fad was for boys to wear long hair.

He never sat in a barber chair, because I was the barber for all three boys.

Babyhood was cut short for Buddy, because a baby sister arrived soon after he was a year old. I was afraid I might fall, or drop him as I carried him up, or down the stairs. The solution was to teach him how to climb the stairs. At eight months, I positioned him on his knees, and showed him how to pat the next step three times with his hand, and then pull himself to a standing position. He then put his knee on the next step; pat, pat, pat, he repeated the process. He was a fast learner, and soon learned the process of coming down the stairs, too, also using the three pats for reassurance.

Often a patient saw him crawl down the hall, and start to climb the stairs; they would run and grab him. Ironically, he was the only child that never fell down the stairs.

Barefoot, four-year-old Buddy was riding in the Volkswagen with his dad and two brothers. They saw some baby skunks on the side of the road, and Dad stopped the car. Buddy said, "Do you think they have their stinkers yet?"

His dad said, "I don't know."

Buddy climbed from the backseat, and got out of the car. He proceeded slowly toward the skunks. Suddenly, he screamed, and ran back toward the car calling out, "Yes, they do!"

His brothers made him ride the rest of the way with his foot outside the window.

The kids were like every other family; they had their fights, but they were the first to defend, and protect each other. We lived close to the railroad tracks, and the whistle was very loud. The girls were scared when they heard the train whistle; they covered their ears, and ran to Buddy so we could hold, and protect them. When they got older they still ran just to stand near him.

Billy was over three and one-half years older than John, and John was two years older than Buddy. Billy ruled John, so John ruled Buddy. Buddy remembers John getting after him. Buddy ran for the patient's bathroom, because it was the only room in the house that had a lock. Buddy slammed the door, pushed the button to lock it, and yelled, "Mamma, Daddy, Mamma, Daddy!"

John had a nail, and he pushed it in the hole in the door knob to unlock it. Buddy had to be ready to push the button to lock it again. Buddy told me, "He beat the snot out of me when he got ahold of me, but at school if someone was picking on me, he was my defender, and he beat the snot out of them. Once they were gone, then he could beat me up. All of us boys were our sisters' protectors."

Buddy's descriptions of some events of his youth:

We used to snowmobile in Hamilton's field near the house. Terry was quite little and she said, "I can't make it. I can't make it home." She was really cold. It was snowing hard; I took off my coat, and put it on her, and helped her home. Another time we were dragging Scotte's sled behind the snowmobile on the crust. She flipped upside down, and was scraped, and scarred up pretty badly.

Friday afternoon the train dropped off a boxcar to be loaded with bags of shavings from Hammond's Lumber Mill on Monday. The neighborhood kids felt they could use the boxcar until Monday morning. Somebody asked Buddy, "Where are they shipping the shavings and what are they going to do with them?"

He told them, "They are being shipped to Cape Canaveral to be used in the monkey cages of the monkey they shoot to the moon." Bud said, "I don't know where I got that idea."

Bud tells: out behind Hammond's Mill there was a huge pile of shavings from the planer. They found a market for the shavings, but it wasn't in the area; it had to be shipped out by rail. The train tracks that ran to Portland were right behind our house. There was an old deserted train depot next to the tracks that offered us protection when playing cowboys and Indians, and a railroad siding to park a boxcar or two.

Billy, John, and I struggled to get the door open on the empty boxcar, climb in, and shut the door all but a crack. Sometimes we posted my youngest sister, Terry, as a guard to warn us of any unwanted grown-ups approaching. We had a super-ball, but in the dark boxcar we couldn't see it. We could hear it bouncing, and we each tried to grab it before the other, even if it meant getting hit by the ball, or our brother's fist.

One time between two box cars there was a flatbed loaded with sand. Time after time we all climbed up onto one corner the boxcar, then we ran, and jumped off the high boxcar landing in the sand. This was a memorable afternoon for me, because I got my first kiss. The other neighborhood kids remembered that afternoon too, because they were confronted by a perverted partially clad classmate.

I was the youngest of the boys. We grew up fast and went from being a baby to knowing it all, and wanting to drive. Billy was exposed to Bunk as a mechanic, and he learned how to build go carts and other things. He taught us as we got older.

All the boys in the neighborhood gathered boards, hammers, and nails. We built a treehouse on the mountain near the gold mine. We didn't have a ladder, but our plan was for Billy to climb the tree to the higher branches where he wanted the treehouse, then another boy climbed up behind him, and then a third boy. I passed up the first 2x4, and they passed it on until Billy could start nailing it in place. We did this board after board until we had it all nailed together.

Mother took all of us to the pond for swimming lessons. The station wagon was full, front seat, back seat, and on top of each other in the back. We had to wait patiently until it was time for our class. When we were able to swim out to the dock, the instructor let us jump off, no matter what age we were. That was our free time to play quietly. The girl that taught Romper room on television was our swimming instructor one year. I thought that was pretty neat.

I remember two train wrecks near Raymond Cotton's house. The minute we got home from school we climbed the mountain so we could watch them work. It was amazing how much they got done while we were in school. There were railroad ties piled on both sides. They brought a crane in on a train, and they worked both ends toward the middle.

It was years before we had a colored television. I must have been eight years old before I realized Bill Cosby was black.

We were not allowed to watch television except an hour on Saturday mornings, Walt Disney, and National Geographic.

A new colored television and snowmobile were delivered within an hour of each other Christmas Eve. Soon after that the *Wizard of Oz* was going to be on television. Mother let us invite the entire neighborhood to watch it in color. She made popcorn for all of us. The next day everyone talked about seeing the *Wizard of Oz* in color.

I had done something bad that day, and I had to sit in the kitchen while everyone else was in the living room. I kept sneaking a peek over the bar, but had to be careful, not to be caught. I missed the first part of it, and then Mother told me I could join the others in the living room. Whatever I did, I never did it again.

Steve Bettencourt, Steve Humphrey, and I took Home Economics. That is why I didn't take the advanced physics my senior year. We made t-shirts using tube material for the body and another piece for the sleeves. I bought some brown corduroy for a vest, and bright orange satin for the lining. I sewed the pieces together and left a small opening at the bottom so I could turn it inside out. I sewed that up by hand, made the buttonholes, sewed on the buttons, and finished it with a buckle on the strap in back. I had my vest finished while the rest of the class was still on step two. I took in a black bear hide which had been tanned, and a deer hide. The teacher helped me make two vests out of leather. There was a bullet hole in the leather and I put that where I made the pocket so it was covered up.

I asked Buddy to tell me what he remembered about his Grandpa Barnes. He was only six-years-old when Grandpa died.

THE APPLES UNDER MY TREE

I can remember spending time in the summers at Long Beach. We puttered around out in the garage. When I got bored doing nothing, I went into the house. He knew what I was going to do. I was going to sit in his chair. He waited until I was curled up comfortably in his chair, and then he would sneak in and say, "Get the dickens out of my chair!" Actually, Grandpa's vocabulary was more colorful, but I knew what he meant.

Grandpa took an old muzzle loader, cut it down, and built a small cradle for it. He took the wheels off a toy army truck, and converted these parts into a little toy cannon. He filled it with black powder, put the fuse from a fire cracker down where the cap went, and lit it. The blast made the cannon shoot back a couple feet.

He had built a large toy boat, to scale, for my daddy when he was small. It had a mast, sails, and all the rigging. There was a little cabin on it with tiny men. On a calm day we took this boat down to the lake near where the boats were anchored. The rudder worked, and he set it so the boat curled back around to us. We did this when there was not enough breeze to blow it off course.

When I was really little Grandpa had a trap line out behind their house, and Grandma took me out in the woods to check it. Grandma buckled little snowshoes on me which my great-great-grandpa, Mellie Dunham, had made for my dad, and we walked the trap line. Grandma was chattering the whole time about the woods, and the little animals; she was teaching this little boy the things he needed to learn, so he would love and appreciate nature.

Grammy used to rub Grandpa's hair. He didn't have a lick of hair, but he liked to have his head rubbed. Then she would come and rub mine. To this day I miss that a lot. My son, Wyatt, will come and rub my head, and after a while he will say, "Is that right Daddy?"

I asked Buddy to tell me what he remembered about his Grandpa and Grandma Freese.

I guess the first memory was when Grandpa and Grandma came to Maine on their motorcycle. We put a tent up in the front yard so they could sleep in our beds. It was a really big deal for us to tent out overnight.

One morning he sat visiting with Mother and Dad at the breakfast table, and I kept tugging and tugging at his shirt, pestering him for a motorcycle ride. He said in a deep, strong, authoritative voice, "You sit there and be quiet, and you watch my ears. When you see pancakes coming out my ears, then I will give you a ride." I remember sitting right down waiting for the pancakes to grow out his ears.

I was the youngest boy, and the girls were younger. Grandpa took each of us for a ride either to the watering tub on Bull Ring Road, or to Rattlesnake Pond and back. He took the girls on the smooth straight paved road to Rattlesnake Pond, but the boys wanted to go up Bull Ring Road, because it was winding and hilly. I was so little my feet barely hung off the seat. Grandpa was so big I couldn't reach around him, so I held onto the railing on the seat, and rode with my eyes pinched closed all the way. I was scared to death, and I wasn't happy until I got off, but I begged to ride again.

Grandma was always very sweet, never harsh at all. We often went to see them in Ohio on our April vacation. One summer we were there, and Grandpa picked a big pan of strawberries from his garden; Grandma made biscuits for strawberry shortcake. Grandpa said, "Take some more strawberries. I don't want to see any biscuits." He was my favorite pal.

We used to have a lot fun at their house. I remember it was great fun when Uncle John let us play with his train set.

Bicycle

This is another story told to me by Buddy:

My oldest brother, Bill, got a brand new bicycle, so he gave his old bicycle to John, and John passed his old bicycle on to me. This was one of the happiest days of my life. I was about six years old, and did not know how to ride a bicycle. I was content to just push my new bike around, or sit on it. I needed to be next to an empty wooden Pepsi box up in the garage, or next to the stump over by the ball field. I had to rest one foot on something up off the ground to be able to sit on my bike. There were no such things as training wheels in our town. We only saw them on television, or on the new bicycles at a Sears's store. That is why I was happy to just push my new bike around our end of town. Even if I was brave enough to get up on my bike, and push off from the stump at the ball field, my legs were barely long enough to reach the bottom of the peddle stroke to keep it going.

Uncle Dick was living with us in Maine at that time. He took me to the top of our tarred driveway, just outside the garage, and he said, "Buddy, today I'll help you get your *brave*, and teach you how to ride your bike."

Already, I felt much more confident. I had other offers, but because I was afraid of falling, I avoided their help. But with Uncle Dick, there was no getting out of it. He told me, "Get your peddle halfway up, sit on the seat, and now push back on your peddle as you go down the driveway so you will go slow enough for me to keep up with you, but not so slow that you stop and fall over. At the end of the driveway I want you to turn right, and pedal as hard as you can."

Uncle Dick took ahold of the seat; off I went down the driveway, and around the corner pedaling as hard as I could. I was part way around the avenue, and I looked back at the garage, and saw Uncle Dick standing in the doorway, waving, with a big grin on his face. I was a little upset for a split second, and then I realized I was riding all by myself, and he did not have ahold of the bicycle!

I have used what I learned that day my whole life, and have charged into everything I do. Sometimes the worst part of a job is dreading it. Thank you Uncle Dick.

Life Insurance

None of us can crawl into the mind of an eight-year-old boy to know what he is thinking, or how he reasons. I finally heard this story from Buddy fifty years after it happened.

When the children were young an aggressive insurance salesman explained to us if we bought life insurance on our children at a very, young age it would be much less expensive than if we waited until they were older. He had a policy they could add to when they reached the age of twenty, and again every ten years at this lower rate. We were convinced, and signed up all six children.

A date was set for us to take all the children to Portland for a physical examination before the policies could be completed. Buddy was so proud, and excited about this trip, because none of his playmates had this thing called life insurance. He felt very special. After we got home the neighborhood children were playing on the mountain, several of them climbed up into the tree house. Buddy stood at the open door, and said to Kenny, "Push me out."

Kenny said, "No, you'll get hurt."

Buddy replied, "I can't get hurt, because I have life insurance."

Middle Finger

This night was the night I was going to learn about the "middle finger". My brothers, eight-year-old John and eleven-year-old Billy, knew about the "middle finger", and now it was time for six-year-old Buddy to learn. John sat in the upstairs hallway close to the boy's bedroom, Billy was on the other side just inside the bathroom, and I was sitting at the top of the stairs. I could look down into the waiting room. A little boy and his mother were sitting on the bottom steps, because every chair was taken in the waiting room. He looked up at me, and my brother said, "Stick up my middle finger at him, but don't let anybody catch you." So, this little boy and I were eyeing each other, and when the coast was clear I stuck up my middle finger. He looked at me, and then at his mother, and I could see he told her something. I sat on my hands, and smiled when the mother looked up at me. Now, she was talking to her son.

A few minutes later I gave the little guy the middle finger again. He grabbed his mother's sleeve, and whispered to her. Finally, she told the little boy to stop looking up at me. My brothers were giggling; they thought it was a big lark. Evidently, she ratted me out when she got into the office. My mother never said a word, but the next morning after breakfast as I was ready to leave for school my mother took me aside and said, "Honey, I understand you're having a problem with your fingers. Come into the office with me."

I didn't know what was going to happen. I didn't know what the middle finger meant. She took one of those huge tongue depressors that were six inches long, and taped it twice to my middle finger and twice to the palm of my hand and my wrist, and then she did the same to my other hand.

She admonished me saying, "Don't you take this off all day long." I remember sitting in school with both middle fingers taped to the wooden tongue depressors.

I have never, never ever, ever given the middle finger since then.

My mother was not the only one that knew how hand out punishment that fit the crime.

Years later Debbie gave me a hickey on my neck, and when I came home my dad saw it. I didn't know anything about it, I didn't know what she was doing, but Dad was so upset he made me wear a neck tie to school. I was so embarrassed, and ever since then I have never written on myself, no tattoos, and no marks on my body. Those were two punishments that stuck with me my whole life.

Music

Mom is going to tell you about my musical career.

John played the trumpet and Mr. Fuchs, a skilled musician, came to the house to give lessons. He was looking for more students to participate in the elementary band at Fryeburg, and he asked John to join. I couldn't leave the other children home alone, so everyone went to band practice with John. Rather than just sitting there, trying to be quiet, Buddy found some drum sticks to bang together, and he ended up playing the drum.

The band did not have a trombone player. Mr. Fuchs found an old trombone in a battered case and we bought it for Buddy; he was about six years old. He was so little he couldn't reach the sixth position, but he figured out that a tone half way between the first and second position produced a pitch pretty close to the sixth position. He learned how to improvise at a young age. After a few lessons he was playing trombone in the band, and his sister, Scotte, was playing clarinet.

The band practiced every week and they improved. There was no money for uniforms, so the mothers were asked to purchase white pants and shirts. They marched at North Fryeburg and Hiram on Memorial Day. They also marched at the Fryeburg Fair every year.

By the time Buddy was nine-years-old and in the fourth grade, his trombone playing was very good.

Mr. Dutil, the music director for the new consolidated high school, was devoted in organizing a high school band. He had the students come to the school for band practice during summer vacation to get them ready. John had band practice and all of the kids were home on vacation. I commanded, "Buddy, grab your trombone, you're going with John to play in the band."

He said, "But Mom, I…"

"You, go!"

I often did not have time to take them to the school, so if I spotted a patient in the waiting room that lived near the school I would ask them, "Can you take John and Buddy to the high school for band practice?" When they agreed, they were seen immediately by the doctor even though they were the last ones to arrive. Little Buddy was terrified when a stranger took them to Sacopee High School. He worried like crazy. He wondered how they were going to get home, or would they be lost forever.

John asked the music director for the trombone part for the songs they were going to be playing, while Buddy took his trombone out of the tattered case. Mr. Dutil was pleased to have Buddy play with the band, because there were no trombones.

He was amazed with Buddy's ability to take music he had never played before, and hit every note. He was so excited about Buddy's playing that he went to the superintendent of the district and said, "This boy needs to be at Sacopee Valley at 2:15 every Tuesday and Thursdays for band practice." The bus driver was instructed to go to the Hiram School, and pick up Buddy and his trombone, to drive him to the high school every Tuesday and Thursday. Lawrence drove the bus up the school house hill to Mt. Cutler School, and the principle went to Buddy's room and said, "Buddy you have to go." He grabbed his trombone and jacket, and head for the bus. He felt like a big cheese, because his classmates had another thirty-five minutes of school. At the high school he got off the bus, and climbed three stories up the stairs to the band room. He was always the first one there. Buddy played with the Sacopee band for eight years.

Magician

Somebody in Cornish organized a talent show. While I was helping the three girls choreograph their dance routines Buddy asked, "What is my talent?"

I responded, "It is your mouth and quick wit." I sat at the ironing board with pencil and paper jotting down jokes for him to tell. Doc tried to help, but I had to delete his jokes as they were not appropriate for a seven-year-old boy.

His skit went something like this: He nervously pulled his little red wagon loaded with props onto the stage. Under his left arm he had Diane's little white fury kitten. (You will read more about this kitty later.) As he held the kitty high he said, "I went fishing the other day and caught a catfish." The audience could clearly see a fish tail and fins sewed to the kitty. When the laughter died down he put the catfish in the wagon.

He took a step forward and said, "I went with my daddy on a house call the other day. He told me to stay in the car while he went in to check Mr. Jack, the owner of the hotel. Pretty soon he came out, got a screw driver, and went back inside. In a few minutes he came to the car, and got a hammer. I asked 'Is Mr. Jack going to be okay?'"

He said, "I don't know, I don't have my bag open yet." Buddy knew the audience was his when the laughter died down, and then he told a couple more jokes. For his finale he took a top hat and drumstick from his wagon, and told the audience, "I always wanted to be a magician. I will wave my magic wand over this hat and a rabbit will appear." Magic words and waving of the drumstick followed, "Abra-ka-dabra." Nothing. He tried again. "Skittle-de-doo." Still no rabbit. He tried one more time. "Abra-ka-dabra, skittle-de-doo." When the rabbit did not appear, in frustration, he raised the hat high over his head, and turned it over to place on his head. When he did this raisins flew all over the floor. He shook his hat and declared, "I knew he was in there sometime!" He grabbed the handle to his wagon and pulled it off stage, as he listened to roaring laughter and applause.

I was back stage; panic set in, because the floor was covered with raisins, and the next act was a group of tap dancers. There was going to be a sticky mess. The floor had to be swept, but the broom was on the other side of the stage. The Emcee said, "I'll handle it." She crossed the stage; she came back with the broom, and little Buddy in close pursuit. He grabbed the broom, danced around the stage, and violently swept the raisins into the audience, and onto the laps of the judges. The floor was clean, but he lost his chance of winning a prize to the laps full of raisins.

The next year Buddy and I worked on his skit for the talent show. After many attempts we decided he could play his trombone, but Buddy's best talent was his humor. We put together a skit that had him visiting a friend at an army base. The bugler became ill, and Buddy volunteered to replace him. When it was time for the troops to get up in the morning he put the trombone to his lips and played Reveille, for mess call he played Taps, for assembly he played Retreat, etc. After the laughter died down he played a couple songs.

When the Fryeburg elementary band played at a music concert, he also performed his skit. He received a letter from a business man in Fryeburg. It said, "I have attended many of these concerts over the years, but your skit was the best. I will never forget your humor. Good luck."

Fishing

When Buddy was young he used to go fishing in the brook near Clarence Douglas'. He came home excited about the trout he caught.

He was in Cotton's Store trying to decide how to spend his money on goodies when he noticed a rubber worm in the fishing lure section of the store. He thought that was a great invention. He gave up the candy bars to buy the worm.

He carried the tackle box Grandpa Barnes had given him across the bridge to the small pond next to Dan Hester's house. Inside the box was everything a fisherman would ever need. He fastened the rubber worm onto his line, and cast it out. It got caught on a lily pad, and when he tried to yank it loose he broke his fish line. That really bothered him, because he could see the worm, but couldn't get it. He had just spent his hard earned money on that worm, and he didn't want to lose it. So, he hooked a big daredevil lure onto the fish line and cast it out as close to the worm as he could, and then reeled it back in slowly. He did this again and again; when he thought the daredevil was hooked around the worm he gave his line a yank, and the lure snapped back, and caught him in the arm.

This little boy thought he was a professional fisherman; he calmly took the scissors out of the tackle box, cut the fish line, and then put everything back in his tackle box. He reeled in his empty line, crossed the main road by Lamont's gas station, and walked across the bridge toward home. He kept his composure as he sat quietly in the living room. His folks were working in the office. His mother passed through the living room a couple of times, and finally she asked, "What are you doing in here on such a nice day?" He broke down and started crying, and then he told her he had a fish hook in his arm. It only took his dad a couple minutes to push the hook through, cut off the barb, and remove it.

Cotton's store had a limited number of lures. Buddy acquired most of his collection from his dad. Buddy watched for a patient to come into the office to have a fishhook removed. He would stand there eyeballing the lure. Many of these had three-pronged hooks, but perfectly acceptable to Buddy with the two remaining hooks after Doc had cut one away. The patients were happy to be rid of the hook; they forgot all about the lure, and before they went out the front door, Buddy was going out the back door with his brand new lure. Many of these were fancy expensive lures.

One Sunday, six-year-old Buddy went ice fishing with his dad at Horseshoe Pond. He caught a big bass, but his dad made him throw it back, because it was not legal to catch bass for another month. A week later, in the same pond, his five year old sister, Scotte, caught a huge pickerel. She worked and worked to get him on the ice. Buddy was there to help her pull in the big catch, and take out the hook. He was getting ready to throw it back in the water, because he thought you were supposed to throw all the big ones back. He heard his dad yelling, "No, no!" His dad assured him Scotte's pickerel was legal. Buddy didn't quite understand that rule.

Buddy and Scotte claimed that hole to be theirs, and off limits to grown-ups.

School

Buddy's schooling started in a three-room school house with three grades for each teacher. Kindergarten was only half a day. Miss Gray worked with them first, and when they were working on their assignment, she then worked with the first grade. She had a three foot tall Dick and Jane book (oops I almost forgot Spot), and when she opened it up it was about four feet wide up on an easel. All the students had the same book, but smaller. Then she worked with the second grade. Buddy got A+ in sand box. He learned to play quietly, and cause the teacher no problem, and she let him play in the sand box all morning. I was so busy with the three girls at home plus the office, and other duties I never noticed Buddy was not bringing home papers. His grade card was good, and no complaints from the teacher.

When Buddy advanced to the third grade he had a teacher new to the district. She did not show the ability to push Buddy to his limit, so he continued to coast even without the sandbox.

Buddy tells:

Finally, Russell, Paul and I made it to the fifth grade. I was so excited, because the fifth grade kids had larger seats. I remember the first two weeks we had to take bag lunches, because they didn't have the cafeteria ready. I was sitting in my big, fifth grade seat eating from my bagged lunch, and Mrs. Bachman said, "Buddy will you come up here?" I sat in a chair next to her desk. She put her arm around me and said, "Your mom and I have been talking, and we talked with Mrs. Twitchell. Your spelling needs some help, and we thought it would be easier if you and your sister, Scotte, had the same spelling words, so we are going to put you back in the fourth grade." That crushed me, mostly because I wouldn't be able to sit in the big seats. I had to go back to the small seats. I was really upset. I pretended to do the fourth grade work, but I was listening to the fifth grade work, because this was where my friends were, and I thought I should be in the fifth grade. It didn't matter, because I still got to leave school on Tuesday and Thursdays to go to band practice.

I remember when I was in the middle room, the entire school went to the sixth grade room to watch them blast off to the moon.

Buddy just told me the following story:

My boss at Trico in the paper mill where I am working now said, "Boy, you're going to have to get some new shoes because you are running back and forth so much."

I shuddered and snapped at him, "Say to and fro from now on!"

In a shaking voice he repeated, "Okay, to and fro."

I told him, "You see I was in the fifth grade for about two week and my teacher thought I should go back 'n fourth, and whenever I here 'back 'n forth', I shudder uncontrollably." He got a big kick out of that. Whenever I am walking through the mill, and I see him at a distance I yell, "To and fro!"

Margaret tells: I was bringing a carload of seventh graders home from soccer practice, and every one of them said they had been put back, and it was a good thing for them. Buddy said, "It made a big difference in sports." I was born in December and in the eighth grade basketball, and soccer I had at least a half years growth ahead of the kids we played against. I was one of the big kids, and it gave me a chance to excel in the sports. I was on the Jr. Varsity basketball team only one year, and then I played Varsity. I played Junior Varsity only about three quarters of the game, and then I would go suit up for the varsity team. I didn't play much until near the end of the game.

Buddy was in high school and he asked me, "Is it okay if I skip school?"

I asked, "Do you know what the punishment is?"

He said, "Three days of detention."

I informed him I would not write an excuse or lie for him. I felt it was his decision to make, because he was the one that had to be in detention. He seldom ever skipped school, but one day he did with several other students. The next morning many of them showed up with forged excuses thinking they were fooling the administration. When Buddy stepped up to the desk they asked, "Where were you yesterday?"

He replied, "I skipped school."

"You know you will have to report for detention three afternoons."

"I know; when do I start?"

The principle was anxious for the room to empty, so he could telephone me, and tell me about his honesty.

There is no job more challenging than that of a substitute teacher. Miss Peach would ask who was absent and everybody anxiously donated a name for her list of absentee students. Buddy's favorite name was Fred Tripp. One day we were taking care of patients, and I asked Buddy to come into the office to meet a patient. "This is Fred Tripp." His mouth dropped open. Later he told me he did not know there was a real Fred Tripp.

Broken Bones

Buddy was in the eighth grade playing wing position in soccer. The ball was passed way ahead of him. Running as fast as he could he was able to keep the ball going. He was running so fast no one could catch up to him, so he could pass it to them. He should have let the rest of the team catch up with him, but what does an eighth grader know. He started cutting toward the middle; it was just Buddy and the goalie. He dribbled too far in front of himself, and the goalie thought he could do a superman dive for the ball, but Buddy stretched out, and kicked the ball as hard as he could. It bounced in underneath the goalie, and Buddy scored the goal and the goalie. The goalie's Superman dive and the force of Buddy's kick caught him in the ribs, and broke Buddy's ankle. Buddy tried to jump up as he scored, but he ended up in a heap on the ground. John leaped from the bleachers, and tore to the aid of his injured brother. John determined his dad could take care of the fracture at home, and refused to let anyone call the rescue unit.

They loaded Buddy into Helen Harrington's car and she brought him home. Doc put a cast on his right leg from just below his knee to his toes.

At this time he was riding his Honda 350 motorcycle to school. It had a sissy bar on the back of it. He stood his crutches upside down, and using a bungee cord he strapped them to the sissy bar. He straightened out a coat hanger with the hook at the top, and duct taped it to the inner part of his cast. He slid the hook over the shifting lever, and just pushed down on it when he wanted to down shift.

He hid his Honda across the river at Delmar's, and shoved up next to the garage, so we didn't know he was riding it to school each day.

He was a sophomore the second time he broke his ankle. It was the first time they played soccer under the lights at Gorham. His teammate passed the ball, and again it was way in front of Buddy; he was running to get it. Buddy saw a Gorham player was going to get to the ball first, so he jumped up in the air putting out his arms, and did everything he could to block him. The ball hit Buddy right in the face, his head went back, and his feet went out in front of him. His cleats caught in the ground, and rolled his ankle back under him. The break was bad enough that Doc put a full-leg cast on him, all the way to his thigh.

This year he was riding Grandpa Freese's big Harley motorcycle. He attached a clothes hanger to his cast like before, so he could shift the bike.

Buddy and another motorcycle rider came up over Cornish Station Hill; they were going to turn right to go to East Baldwin. He came down the hill toward the intersection and saw nothing was coming, so he turned right. Before they got over the next hill Dave Lombard, a state policeman, pulled up behind them. Buddy told me, "It seems like Dave lived in our trunk or our saddle bags, because whenever we did something wrong he caught us. He pulled us over, and gave both of us a ticket for running a stop sign."

Buddy already had a couple tickets, and he was afraid this ticket might cause him to lose his license, so instead of paying the fine he went to court. The judge asked, "How do you plead?"

Buddy said, "Nolo contendere."

She asked, "What do you mean?"

He answered, "Well, I did stop at the stop sign, but I didn't put my foot down. On a motorcycle a complete stop is considered when you put your foot down."

She said, "Put your foot down, what are you talking about?"

"Well, when you are riding on a motorcycle you are supposed to put your foot down when you stop."

She could not find anywhere on the ticket where it said motorcycle. She called Dave to the stand, "Show me where it says motorcycle." He pointed, but his writing was like chicken scratching, and she gave him the dickens about his writing.

Buddy again told her he had stopped, and then made his turn.

She said, "Why didn't your friend stop?"

"I waved him through when I saw the road was clear. Yes, legally I did not stop, because I didn't put my foot down, but I did stop, and I am not guilty."

"Why didn't you put your foot down?" Now Buddy was scared. He wondered what was going to happen to him when Dave, and the judge found out he was driving wearing a cast.

"My foot was in a cast and the other foot was my brake foot. I was on a hill, and I didn't dare put that foot down, because I would start rolling again."

She let him go. He only had to pay the court costs.

Deer on Motorcycle

Dad and I went hunting on the mountain early in the morning. We started hunting in the valley and worked our way up, and then we moved back down, and did another hunt. It was time for office hours. Dad said, "If we hurry we have time for one more hunt. Run down beyond the Frenchman's camp, cut into the next road, and get on a good deer crossing."

Back then the trees were so thick because of the fire twenty-five years earlier. Now you can get across anywhere. I ran down to where I could see fairly well. There were bushes everywhere. I heard a crashing noise coming toward me. I thought it must be Dad, late for office hours making such a racket. Then he stopped just before I could see him. I thought oh my goodness that might be a deer. Suddenly, he took off from my left. I could see it was a deer, but I didn't know if it was a buck. So, I pulled up ahead with my gun resting against a small tree. As I peered through the scope I saw movement. I didn't squeeze the trigger; I yanked it. I took off running parallel to him. I knew there was a corner by the road, and I thought I could beat him to the corner before he crossed the road. I went about thirty yards, and I twisted my ankle. Dad had just taken off my cast. I fell down in a big heap. I kept the gun in the air so I didn't bang the scope, and I hobbled back to where I had shot. Daddy hooted and I hooted back rather quietly, because I missed the deer.

I stood where I was when I pulled the trigger, and located the opening where the deer was when I shot. I was looking for the tree I hit. Dad hooted again and I called "Over here." I went a little further, and then I saw some blood. Now, I started hollering to Dad that I got him. I ran down and found the deer. He was stuck under a tree. I pulled and pulled. Finally, I got his head out and saw he had antlers. We dressed him out, and dragged him a little ways to a blow-down-tree close to the brook I had crossed earlier. We shoved him in under the blow-down, and covered him with leaves. We didn't have time to get him out of the woods because of office hours.

We came home, and Dad told me I would have to go back, and get him out by myself. I went and got Danny Eastman on my little 350 Honda that I just bought that summer. I drove the bike all the way up the mountain, and out the trail almost to the brook. I parked the bike there, and crossed the brook searching for the deer. He was well hidden, but we finally found him. We dragged him out, and crossed the brook with great care so as not to get the cavity wet. It took a lot of pulling and tugging, but we finally got him to the Honda.

It was a big deer. We tried to get him up onto the seat of the 350, but the bike would fall over, or the deer would fall over. We weren't very big kids, anyways we gave up. I tied the deer to the motor cycle, and started dragging it. I dragged it until there was not a speck of hair left on that side of the deer. We continued down the mountain toward Clarence's to where there was an old vehicle next to the road in the woods. Trees had grown up around it. The fenders stuck out fifteen inches from the car. We dragged the deer over to the old car, and got him up on the front fender. Then we pulled the motorcycle backwards through the bushes, and next to the car. We pulled, and tugged until we got the deer half on the fender, and half on the bike. We wrapped him around the sissy bar, and tied him up with all of the rope we had. The deer slid off the fender of the car as we pushed the bike out onto the road. I sat on the gas tank, and Danny sat on the deer. We rode the bike to the tagging station. Danny had to stand there and hold up the bike, because the kick stand couldn't hold all that weight.

Jobs

I had many jobs as I was growing up in the little country town in Maine.

Hunk Ward lived in the old Mt. Cutler Hotel next to Cotton's store. He made some money repairing broken wooden Pepsi or Coke cases. They would drop off a truckload of broken cases in his yard for him to repair. Hunk wanted to spread the wealth, and the work around, so he paid the kids three cents to replace a metal binding and five cents to replace an end. The end pieces had slots in them to act as handles. We took apart badly broken boxes to retrieve an end. I was eight years old when I worked on these boxes. I worked until I made twenty-five cents; once I had that money I headed for Cotton's store. At that time twenty-five cents would buy a soda and two candy bars, or two ice cream sandwiches. I bought them, and took them under the bridge to eat, because I knew if my mother caught me eating them, I would be in trouble for squandering my money.

One time Mother caught one of the kids, about four years old, with a candy bar; she asked him where he got it. The final verdict was he had stolen it. She marched him right over to Mr. Cotton, and made him confess to the crime, and to ask if he could work off the debt. Mr. Cotton started to say, "Oh, that's ok..." when she interrupted and said it was not okay. She thought the thief should sweep the porch, empty the wastebaskets, and do other chores for a week to repay him. He realized the child needed to learn from their mistake, and to my knowledge they never took another candy bar.

My folks had twenty acres of blueberries in Upton. Dad tried to burn the fields every other year to produce a better crop. You will see the recurring stories of picking blueberries. It was mandatory or slave labor; except we got to keep the money from the berries we picked unless mother grabbed us by the ear, and marched us to the bank to deposit it in our savings account.

Buddy's first job away from home was working at Camp Blazing Trail, a girl's camp sponsored by the Boston YWCA. There were about 200 girls in the two adjoining camps. He was twelve years old, and two weeks had passed since his brother, John, left to work there. He was disappointed he couldn't go with John, but when they were hiring at the end of the previous summer I did not think Buddy was ready to assume the duties, so they hired a seventeen year old boy. This boy stole money from John's dresser, and when the camp director caught him smuggling in cigarettes for the girls, she fired him.

The director called, and I told her Buddy had matured greatly over the winter, and I felt he could handle the job, but I wanted her to really lay down the law, and talk with him. Lyn came to the house; she sat with Buddy, and talked for a long time about the big responsibility. He came to me to get permission. I was hesitant, saying, "I don't know, that is a very big responsibility." He begged, promising he would do a good job. I handed him a box of folded clean clothes, and wished him well. He was so excited he never wondered why the clothes were ready and waiting for him. This was the first time he would be sleeping in a tent all night away from home.

He hopped in the car with Lyn, and it seemed like the ride took forever to get to camp, because he was so anxious to get to work. That was a good summer; John hand washed dishes in the kitchen, and then he washed the pots and pans outside of the senior camp. He had a great time spraying any girls that paused to tease him. Buddy's job was to get out the supplies needed for the next meal, and wash the pots and pans at the junior camp. As soon as either boy finished, he raced through the woods to help the other finish their chores. (Percy had trimmed a good trail between the two camps). They had the afternoon off, and would either sign out flippers and facemasks, or a canoe and paddles.

The next summer he was right back at Blazing Trail. John had a new job working at Simpson's Beach on Sebago Lake. Buddy worked at the junior camp and Kenny Richardson worked at the senior camp. He made $200.00 for the summer, and he put most of it in the bank. Buddy was in trouble with the cook for one of his pranks. The pancakes were ready to go on the griddle, and the cook went to the restroom before she started this huge task. When she was out of sight, Buddy poured green food coloring into the batter. Granny was livid, and the campers loved it. Buddy spent the morning flipping flapjacks while granny rested in the corner with a smile on her face.

Buddy tells of a prank they pulled on one of the campers.

One girl was being disciplined for her bad behavior. That night they made her stand by a big tree at the edge of the woods. The boys heard about it. As darkness set in Kenny and I went out with a flashlight, and snuck in behind her, I turned on the flashlight kind of close to her eyes so she couldn't see who it was. I stuck out three fingers in front of her, and said in a spooky voice, "I'm three fingered Willie."

Kenny chirped, "And I am one eyed Sam." That little black girl turned as white as a sheet.

John worked at Simpson's Beach snack bar for the last two summers. The third year before summer work started he took Buddy to be interviewed by Larry Simpson; Larry hired Buddy to work the Fry-o-later, and John to work the grill again, like he had done the year before. All the summer vacationers got to know John.

A couple weeks later John was killed in an automobile accident. Larry promoted Buddy to John's job out front on the grill with the hamburgers, hot dogs, and steamed rolls.

Buddy looked enough like his brother that the summer customers called him John, and after a few weeks his ulcer started acting up. This caused Buddy feelings of extreme sadness.

Buddy walked to work as he lived with Grandma Rose Barnes the two years he worked at Simpson's snack bar. He was fifteen years old, but he was working four shifts over ten hours per day, and two eight-hour shifts a week. He had one day off and was paid $1.70 per hour. He didn't have much of a social life except for the kids he worked with. They were a great bunch of kids and he is still close to them.

The greasy air particles bothered his ulcer, and when he got home the last thing he wanted was anything greasy. Grandma would have potatoes all mashed up, corn, and good meals every night. He went to Bingo with her on Wednesday evenings. Buddy reminisced, "She was a wonderful grandma, and it was a good place to live. I remember she looked fail and skinny."

The first motorcycle he bought was a used Honda 350. He had saved one hundred fifty dollars, but the asking price was three hundred fifty dollars. Grandma loaned him two hundred dollars, and by the end of the third week he had paid off the loan. She was very proud of him.

The following year when Buddy was seventeen years old, he lied about his age to work on the Cornish Limerick road construction. He told them he was eighteen. The road was just about finished; they were painting lines. They dumped gravel any place there was a culvert for access to a field, and the men dressed the culverts with stones, and then spread the gravel. That job lasted about three weeks, and they laid everyone off, but the old foreman called Buddy aside, and asked him to come back for one more week to do the final touches. He chose Buddy because when they were told to do a job, he was right there doing it, and the others did as little as they could. The old man told Buddy, "Stay away from those boys, they're no good."

The year before Buddy had bought a Honda 350, and he was going to take off the rest of the summer to ride his motorcycle. He had been making $2.70 per hour. The last day he finished about one o'clock and came home. He stopped by the waiting room to visit with patients, and Lois Metcalf asked, "What are you up to?"

"I just finished working on the Limerick Road and I'm going to ride my bike the rest of the summer. I've been working for five years, and I finally got a vacation."

An old man, blind in one eye, sitting over in the corner of the waiting room asked him, in a rather loud voice, "Are you looking for a job?" He definitely wasn't, but Buddy knew if his dad heard him refuse a job, he would be in deep do-do.

Buddy asked, "What do you have?"

He replied, "Operating an Italian bulldozer, $3.00 to start."

Buddy thought, boy, that's a lot of money; to start means there might be a raise in it. Running a piece of equipment, WOW, he was excited. He said, "Of course!" That sounded pretty neat!

He told Buddy to show up at his place in Denmark at six o'clock Monday morning. So there he was all 115 pounds of him, showing up on his 350 Honda ready to go. It turned out that operating an Italian bulldozer was wheeling a wheelbarrow of wet, heavy cement into the basement of a house in Bridgton.

Concrete

Buddy relates the following events:

They stuck a chute through the basement window, and filled a wheelbarrow with 350 pounds of cement. I had to wheel it across the dirt floor. I remember the first day they would say, "Okay, go." I made up my mind I was going to do it; I grabbed the handles of the wheelbarrow and started pushing. The floor was sandy, and I couldn't do it. The wheelbarrow flipped over on its side spilling its contents long before its final destination. The old guys laughed, and scraped the cement out of the way, and a couple other guys took their loads to the other end. Now, it was my turn again. I grabbed ahold, and got my wheelbarrow almost where I was the first time, and it tipped over again. Somebody yelled, "That's okay we need some there, too." Before long we had the job done, and we climbed out of the window.

The day they hired me they also hired a boy from Brownfield, two years older and twice my size. At the end of the first day, he said, "I'm quitting; this isn't for me." He just didn't like working. I had already decided that this was my last day too, but on the way home I decided I would stay another day so I could say I outlasted him, and he couldn't tell his parents I quit too. I wanted to make them think I was a little tougher than I was.

The next day the blind guy, his alcoholic friend, and I were sent up to Minot, Maine; I remember calling home to let Mother know where I was. I had never been so far from home, forty miles. We were working on a cow farm. They backed the cement truck right up to the site and dumped it; we didn't have to move anything. We poured the cement real loose, and the blind guy and his alcoholic friend could drink beer the rest of the day. Where I didn't weigh anything, they put me out on the cement on a couple kneeboards. They taught me how to finish the floor, and I did the entire floor by myself while they lay in the shade drinking their beer, and occasionally yelling, "Good job!"

They thought it was great to have someone drive them around, and to do the finish work while they drank. I finished the rest of the summer doing concrete work, and by the end of the summer I had saved over $950 dollars. I used that money to buy Grandpa's Harley motorcycle.

The next year Ben, the blind guy, and Dan his alcoholic friend weren't with the company, but their partner Dave Nagle started out the next spring when he got back from Florida. He called me up; he had no crew, and it was just Dave and me that summer.

Stopping by the waiting room, and talking with Lois was a big mistake. I could have been an engineer instead.

The next year Dave was busy building a huge kiln near Rumford, Maine. The foundations were poured, and the dirt was in, but before the floor could be poured it all had to be tied with re-bar, a grid six inches on the center. He didn't have enough time to do it, so he hired me, and my crew to do it. I had to find a crew. Andy McClare was around so I grabbed him. I had two dogs and Andy had three. We got a room on the second floor of the hotel. After we got in we came down the fire escape, and smuggled the dogs into the hotel room one dog at a time. It was an old hotel, and everybody used the one bathroom at the end of the hall. It was a very small room. Our window was the same level as the roof of the auto parts store next door. We just opened the window, and the dogs would hop out onto the gravel roof, do their business, and hop right back in. By the third day we were tired of the ladder thing. We walked in the main door; the stairway was off to the right. One of us would distract the person watching the door, and we would scramble the five dogs up the stairs.

I worked for that company through high school and college. After college I started building my house and pouring floors on my own.

George and Gene Stacey were so far behind on their construction work, they weren't going to have time to do any hunting. They asked me in late summer if I would help them do carpentering so they could get some time off in November. They didn't let go of me four years.

Doug was starting a foundation company, because that was where the money was. I had taught him how to do floors before that, but now he was so busy doing foundations he couldn't get back to pour the floors so, I started pouring his floors, and soon was doing floors for everyone else. I worked six months doing cement, 6-7 days a week. I would set up my jobs on Sunday, and pour all week. I was making a year and one-half wages in six months.

How did you come up with the name Capt'n Crete?

I poured a lot of concrete in North Conway in the 1970's when it was becoming a tourist mecca. An older man, one hell of a nice guy, drove the truck that delivered cement. When he pulled in he leaned out his window and yelled, "Captain Crete is here." He passed away about the same time as I was starting my business, so in memory of him I used the name Capt'n Crete.

CAPTAIN CRETE
Concrete Floors & Stuff

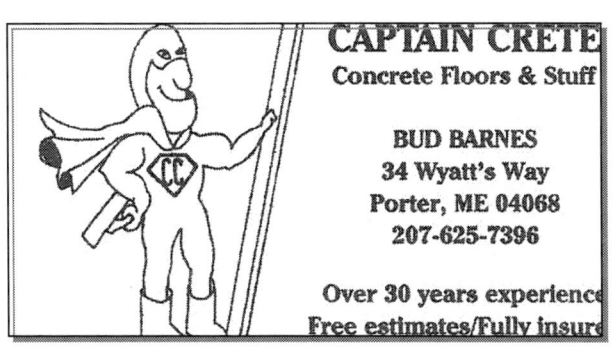

BUD BARNES
34 Wyatt's Way
Porter, ME 04068
207-625-7396

Over 30 years experience
Free estimates/Fully insured

Years later I wanted to have some T-shirts made up, and I needed some kind of super-hero logo. My logo developed as I took the face of the Bud man; he had a cape that came over his head and flowed behind him. I used the chest shield from Superman and put CC on the shield. I had my super hero with big bulging muscles holding a straight edge. Later we made one with the same body and a motorcycle with a flatbed on the side car, hauling a power trowel and coal chute on the bed.

I poured the concrete floors for Carol Noonan when she was creating the Stone Mountain Arts Center. She was impressed by my work and sense of humor, and she wrote and recorded a song about me.

Captain Concrete an Ode to Bud Barnes

Captain Concrete, Captain Concrete
A sweet lament 'bout the king of cement
Captain Concrete
   Oh tarnation, I need a foundation
   Who ya gonna call when you need a wall
   Captain Concrete
A super hero in the cement biz
A concrete scientist is what he is
Captain Concrete, Captain Concrete
   Pours you a slab, he's way super fab
   Captain Concrete
Brought in a mixer, but he had 'a fix'er
Then he started pourin', had to put a floor in
Captain Concrete
   The lady customers all have a fit,
   Because he has a way with aggregate

Captain Concrete
He poured our basement floor in record time
And while he did it, he sang...My Darlin' Clementine!
Captain Concrete, Captain Concrete
Captain Concrete, Captain Concrete
A sweet lament 'bout the king of cement
Captain Concrete, Captain Concrete
Who ya gonna call when ya need a wall
Captain Concrete, Captain Concrete, Captain Concrete

Written and recorded by Carol Noonan

Work Ethics

This is the story Buddy likes to tell at the paper mill; it is about work ethics as a kid.

All of us children were brought up as workers. The girls had to work in the house; Mother took care of them, but we boys worked outside. One day I had to stack the wood Dad had thrown off the truck into the back yard. Dad was on house calls. The neighborhood boys, Kenny and Russell, were riding their bikes around the avenue, calling, "Come on Buddy, come ride with us." I hurried as fast as I could piling the wood so I could go riding with them, climb the mountain, play in the treehouse on the mountain, sabotage the train tracks, or whatever was going on for that day.

Later that day we were riding around the avenue and I saw the Volkswagen in the driveway, and the wood pile laying on its side in the yard. I knew what had happened; I knew Dad had knocked it over. So, I wasn't going to go anywhere near the house until they called me in. Sure enough at lunch-time they caught up with me. Dad took me out, and explained that the wood was piled improperly, some pieces had the split side up instead of the bark side up, and it was so unstable that a small wind could blow it over onto one of the girls or the dogs. He was very ashamed of my work. Then, he wheeled my bicycle up into the barn, and hung it on the wall high above my head. He went to a pile of scrap boards, and he found a board that said *Tuesday* on it, and nailed it under my bike; that was the day I got my bike back. With it firmly nailed to the wall, there was no way I could exchange the board, hoping he would forget; I had to wait until Tuesday. The wood needed to be piled before I could play.

I tell this story to my co-workers at the paper mill. "I didn't like it worth a snot as a kid, because they kept us busy weeding the garden, or if it was a rainy day we had to help clean the house." Mother tried to make us think we were playing a game, she would pick up some misplaced item, and like a dispatcher at the taxi office, she would say, "Taxi, take this to bathroom street, or take this to basement street."

My parents made sure that each day our time was used to accomplish something constructive, but never explained to us why they were making us work while Russell and Kenny were riding around calling, "Let's go, let's go play," and I was working.

The mill people are going, "Oh, my God!"

In the winter in Maine when it was snowing like the dickens, they didn't call off school, because we walked to school. Mother hauled us out of bed before daylight to fulfill our duties before the school bell rang. Billy was old enough to drive the old jeep, and he plowed the foot deep snow away from the driveway. Lucky Bill, I wish I was old enough to drive. John and I had to head out with shovels, not just any shovel, but our Christmas present shovel. We each received a shovel for our Christmas present plus an electric race car set that the three of us had to share. That was okay, because our other Christmas present was wax, so the snow would not stick to the shovel. Off we went like good little obedient soldiers. First we had to shovel out Raymond Cotton's Store; even if it was still snowing we had to do the store before he came to open it up. He was not allowed to pay us, and my folks did not pay us. We were taught the privilege of giving. We would leave there, and go down the road to an elderly lady's house; Anne Spring would give us a quarter when we shoveled out her walk. John was older, and he told me half of a quarter was twelve cents. Then we had to shovel the church, next door, for the Lord. I had no idea what tithing meant, I only knew we did it for free. On the way back home, we shoveled out Maxine's place for a cookie or piece of cake, and then we shoveled out the walk to the doctor's office and no pay for that, just the privilege of eating at the table.

We had the mountain, and a whole neighborhood in which to play, and all the Barnes children knew when they heard the whistle they had to drop everything and head for home. Mother might only want one of us, but we all had to be front and center. Her whistle had two tones giving a harmonic pitch. She kept this silver whistle on the window sill; easily accessible to call in her flock. When we heard one long and two shot blasts, the entire neighborhood knew Margaret was calling. We all responded immediately to the melodious beckoning as we feared the repercussions of not obeying. If she wanted only one of us, she would wave off the others so they could return to their play. Much as we disliked being summoned we never attempted to hide Mother's pager.

My parents made sure we always had chores. In the summer it was weeding the garden, in the fall it was piling wood, but I must also tell you on the hot summer days Mother would load us, and all our neighborhood friends into the station to take us to Rattlesnake Pond to swim and to cool off. Why is it easier for us to grumble than to remember the daily gifts of love and caring? We didn't understand they were teaching us lifelong lessons with each task we were asked, or told to perform.

I had been working away from home since I was twelve years old, just to get away from playing taxi on a nice sunny day. I was paid two hundred dollars for working at Camp Blazing Trail; I did see the check once, but my mother took the money, and put it in the bank. I wanted to buy candy bars and soda pop; I didn't understand that someday I would be able to use this money to buy a motorcycle.

I went on telling the men it wasn't until I went to college that I realized I had cut my parents a little bit short. How could they, growing up in the 1920's and 1930's, understand what a kid was going through in the 1960's? After all we were brilliant kids, and they were like cave people; anyway, that was the way I figured it.

My first week at college, I was getting up at five o'clock in the morning, because that was when my body alarm clock went off. On Saturday morning I am up and out at five o'clock experiencing the world around me, listening to the birds and enjoying life, but I had to wait until two o'clock in the afternoon for my buddies to start rolling out of bed. Then they were up all night, and slept in on Sunday.

The second week, I said, "What a bunch of weirdoes," except for Steven, a boy from Greenville, and Paul Mitchel who grew up working hard in New Bedford. We were chumming around wondering what the heck was wrong with all the other kids.

About the third week I realized there were a lot more kids who slept in than the kids who didn't. It was still another three weeks before I realized the reason we were up in the morning, was not because Dad needed us to shovel the snow or the garden needed weeding, and the wood needed to be piled, but he was getting us ready for life. For instance, my parents did not tie our shoes, they taught us, and we tied our own, so if anything happened to them, we didn't have to wear loafers the rest of our life.

The engineers and officials in the mill enjoyed my stories, as they grew up like I did. They also saw that these stories produced better work from those that had not benefitted from an early work ethic experience.

After the men at the mill heard my story, one of them said, "My brothers, sisters, and I weren't poor; our folks were, and they just dragged us along with them." They grew up working hard too, and they always enjoyed the analogy of my stories.

Motorcycle

This is the story Buddy told me about buying Grandpa's motorcycle.

When I was eighteen, all I had was my Honda 350 motorcycle and I wanted to buy Grandpa's Harley Davidson motorcycle. He wasn't riding it any more. I called him up, and I told him how much money I had, and he said that was fine.

Billy took me out in his truck, and when we got out there, you know what a jokester he was, he told me he had to have twice that amount. I didn't know what I was going to do. He said he had talked with the dealers, and they said it was worth more. By the third day I had accepted the fact that I could not afford the bike.

I was upstairs in their bathroom, looking out the window onto the back yard; I could see the railroad track and a little barn. I saw Billy's truck backed up to a loading dock. Billy and Grandpa were pushing the motorcycle from the barn over to the loading dock. Oh boy! It didn't take me too long to get down those steps, though the yard, and to the loading dock.

When we arrived back in Hiram, we put the motorcycle in the basement of the house. I spent all my extra time taking everything apart, and putting it back together. The seat on Grandpa's motorcycle was vinyl and it was cracked and ripped. I took the seat and a tanned bear-hide to an auto upholstery place to have it recovered. I was so proud of the seat, and I didn't want anything to happen to it. I took the seat off and took it to bed with me every night. I had the motorcycle back together, and it was time to try to start it. The noise it made was earth shattering, and Mother made me move the motorcycle to the barn.

I was playing softball after I built our house and the bike caught on fire when I started it up. I pushed it to the edge of the road and laid it on its side. I scooped up sand and covered it to put out the fire. The lady next door came out with a fire extinguisher, and put out the fire. But it burned long enough that it compromised the leather on the nose of the seat. There was a hole about the size of a quarter. I rode it until four years ago when I restored Grandpa's bike, and then I changed it. I liked that leather seat so much that I almost didn't send the seat to be redone, because I had several seats. But I wanted all the parts on Grandpa's bike to be the originals. Nobody would ever have known except me.

Miscellaneous Stories

I started working in the paper mills in 1994. It made me much more confident about my mechanical ability. Every paper mill in the country has to shut down for a week or two every six months to a year depending upon what specific devise or worn part had to be repaired or rebuilt.

A defuser shoots water into the pulp and pulls the water back out several times until the pulp is rid of the bad chemicals. It is a big screen like a colander. We had to replace, and repair the worn parts. The holes are no bigger than a paper clip. We are replacing sheets of steel twelve feet high. Working with hydraulics, we tear it apart, re-machine it, and get it going again. The cost of the bearings range from $2,000 to $20,000 each. It is like a nine story pressure cooker. A two-foot pipe come into top separator, an auger to push the chips down. The job has taught me a lot about myself that I did not know before.

After Wyatt was born I wanted to spend more time at home, and started pouring concrete on my own. Things were going real well. The ice storm came and I moved my equipment up on the mountain to salvage the damaged trees.

College

You had a friend, Mr. Pompanichalo, how did you meet him?

I was doing the prep work like, baking potatoes, etc. I practically lived there putting in close to twelve hours a day. By the time summer came I was doing the cooking, and they hired another fellow to do the cleaning, dishes, pans, and stuff. Connie Kendall was one of my waitresses. (You will see later how Connie influenced the other children).

While I was in high school I worked at Stone Ridge Restaurant after school and evenings. Soon They hired a pretty girl from Connecticut as the hostess; that was Pappy's daughter. One day at a cookout he told me, "It's okay if you date my daughter, but it's not okay if you aren't going to go to college." He knew how to get a boys attention.

The next day, at his encouragement, I talked with the student advisor, Mr. Delaney. I needed advanced physics, and advanced math to be accepted in college for engineering. I went to high school the next year to take these two classes, plus a four hour lab. I was able to continue working, pouring concrete, etc. plus studying.

The following year I was accepted at Franklin Institute of Engineering in Boston, and University of Maine in Orono. I really didn't want to go to Boston, too many people. When they told me how many kids were in the dorm at Boston, I said, "No way! I am going to Orono."

I was a late acceptance, because I took a year off. That was a red flag, so I had to go to Orono to take a test to prove I was a good enough student to qualify in the math.

I rode Grandpa's bike the day of the examination. I am early like I always am; sitting in the parking lot enjoying the beautiful morning when this boy shows up in a big LTD car. He was there to pick up the first load of stuff from his girlfriend's dorm room. He was a shorter guy, but quite rugged. His dad was a hard working farmer, carpenter, and a do-it-yourself man. He wore a little leather biker cap. I went over to speak to him and he said, "Oh yeah, I have a Harley, too."

I said, "I know, everybody does." I was just picking on him, and that really bugged him. Anyways, we visited quite a while. We both took the test, and stuck around long enough to say, "Catch up with you at orientation." They told us if we passed the test we would have a special orientation in three weeks. Barry said, "I'll bring my bike up then," and I thought, yeah, we'll see. I knew I would have mine whether it was raining or not.

I am early for orientation, and am sitting there when brrrum, brrrum, brrrum here comes Barry on a sporty model, a little bit customized. We hit it off immediately. We both were accepted, but he was housed at Orono. I was in the overflow of late acceptances, and ended up at Bangor Community College which was a series of six three-story, two winged dormitories with rooms on both sides of a central hall. There were three times as many girl dormitories as boys, because most of the classes at BCC had to do with dental hygiene, cosmetology, and nursing.

They shuttled buses every hour between the two campuses. I stayed at Orono for the whole day. After my first two classes at ten o'clock I found an empty engineering room, and did the homework from my first two classes, had another class, eat my lunch there, did my homework after lunch, and then I had one or two classes in the afternoon. They stuffed my schedule full because I was in a 2+2 program. In two years I would have my Associate's Degree, and in two more years I could have a Bachelor's Degree. Most kids were carrying fourteen to eighteen credits; I was carrying twenty-two to twenty-four credits each semester. It helped a lot doing the homework in between the classes.

I was glad my room was in Bangor. One benefit was when I did get a new roommate he usually moved to the Orono campus by the second week. My room was huge, twice the size of the rooms in Orono; I had it all to myself, and the food was better. Other reasons I stayed was there were a lot more girls in Bangor, and I was able to have a vehicle as a freshman at BBC. I made some really good friends there.

Heather

I had an old Volkswagen Bus my second year of college. Dianne, Billy's ex-wife and her daughter Heather were living in a rented apartment in Bangor. Dianne, a nurse, worked three to eleven at the hospital. She was struggling to get by, and babysitting was a big expense for her. I wasn't doing anything but homework, so I told her I would babysit Heather to help her. Some days I would not be back from Orono until forty minutes after she dropped off Heather. All of the boys in my dorm loved me, and they loved Heather too. Dianne dropped her off with whoever had their room open, and said, "Buddy should be right along." This was way before cell phones.

If three-year-old Heather had to pee, I told her before she went into the little boy's bathroom she had to let everyone know. She stood in the hallway, and called out, "Woman in the hall, woman coming in."

Somehow we ended up with a shopping cart in the dorm. A hacksaw removed the basket, except for the handle bars where they went down to the framework. I wired an antique Harley Davidson seats onto the frame. She sat on the seat, put her feet on the frame, and the boys wheeled her up and down the hall.

Soon after I arrived at my room, I took Heather to her apartment, and fixed supper. I started early and worked hard all day; sometimes after supper I dosed off while watching "Mork and Mindy". She never said anything if I fell asleep, because she knew she had to go to bed right after "Mork and Mindy". When I woke up she knew she was in trouble for not being in bed, and she started jabbering right away. "Mork and Mindy" did this and that, and she told me the whole story. She knew if she told me the whole story I wouldn't scold her.

Occasionally, I opened the awning in the Volkswagen van and we had a picnic.

Hunting

The first day of hunting season was on Tuesday. Buddy and a couple of his friends were up at four-thirty heading for the woods before sunrise in hopes of getting a deer. It was still dark, but each boy found a location to their liking, and was waiting for a deer to approach them.

Suddenly, there was a shot. Buddy ran over to the downed deer, and gave a mighty shout of victory. His friends came running. He glanced at his watch. They didn't have much time. He handed his drag rope to Clyde so he could tie it around the deer's antlers while Buddy was busy dressing out the deer with help from Keith. While Buddy washed his hands in a nearby stream, Clyde and Keith unloaded the guns, gathered the clothing, grabbed the rope, and started pulling. Buddy looked at his watch again. There was no time to drive to Clyde's grandfather's farm to hang the deer. They had to return to their dorm, and clean up in time to catch the bus.

As they drove back to Bangor they were proposing suggestions for taking care of the deer. It was going to be a hot day, and they couldn't leave the deer in the car. Tagging the deer would have to wait until after school. They parked, and ran for their rooms. Each boy short sheeted as many beds as they could, and met in Buddy's room. They started tying the sheets together to form a chain, and lowered them out the window, while Buddy and Clyde ran to the car, and dragged the deer through the parking lot, and across the lawn to the place where the sheets were hanging from the window. They attached the rope and sheet together. Buddy ran up the stairs to his room leaving Clyde to lift the deer. In the room, Buddy and Keith started tugging and pulling on the sheets. Slowly the deer ascended the wall. They finally had the deer just below the window. They tied the sheets around the legs of the bed, and cautiously let loose of them. Their chain of sheets was holding.

Rapidly the boys changed clothes, and washed up enough to be presentable. Fortunately, the deer was hanging on the north side of the building, but unfortunately it was clearly visible from the parking lot.

When classes were over, and the bus returned them to their dormitory Buddy found a note taped to his door inviting him to visit the Dean's office. He was apprehensive as he entered, then he was downright terrified when he saw the Dean was a woman!

She was not pleased with the décor below his window, but his ingenuity impressed her enough so she only gave him a warning, and instructions to remove the deer immediately. The boys complied, took the deer to the tagging station, and then to Grandpa's farm to hang it in the barn.

When Dad was in Maine Medical Center one of the nurses said, "I have been in your house lots of times during Fryeburg Fair week. The first thing we did was head to the bathroom, next was grabbed glasses from the cupboard, poured some milk, and then cut a piece of chocolate cake, which was always waiting for us on the kitchen table." The house was open to all of Bud's friends.

It became an annual event for the kids in his class at Orono to meet at his house for Fryeburg Fair; they came from northern Maine, and out of state. When all had gathered they jumped into vehicles, and head for Upton where there were enough beds for them to sleep. The next day they shot down to the fair.

Ice Fishing

The winter after college Buddy and his friend Andy enjoyed ice fishing on Sebago Lake. The water was crystal clear. They walked about three-quarters of a mile on the lake to the Camel's Pasture. This is an elevated area about the size of two football fields covered with rocks of all sizes from football size to the size of a Volkswagen Bug. The depth ranges from five to twelve feet, then drops off to a deep ninety feet. The big fish lay on the bottom in the deep water. Schools of smelts congregate on the Camel's Pasture which in turn lure the togue, cusk, and white fish. They chase after, and feed on the schools of smelt.

Buddy and Andy built a fishing shack on skids. It had tinted-glass machine gun-sized windows, which let in very little light so you can see the bottom of the lake really well, but you can still peek out to see if your traps are okay, or if any game wardens are approaching.

Buddy's eyes twinkled as he relayed the following story:

I remember Andy and I were fishing at the Camel's Pasture. Andy was fishing at 90 feet, and I was fishing at 15 feet jigging through the ice. Andy needed some bait, but I had the bait with me, so I went out to meet him half way. As I neared him I crossed a fissure. (A fissure is a large crack in the ice.) During the night the ice expands causing it to crack, and on a nice warm day the ice contracts; some of those cracks were four inches wide in places.

I looked down through the fissure as I walked by; the water was only four feet deep. I baited my hook, and started banging my lure on the rocks, as I was banging I saw a cusk. They are usually night fish. Then I saw two cusk, then four cusk. Boy, it was exciting! There were so many, I was hitting their heads with my lure. I started pulling them out one after another. Once I had five or six cusk, I saw a white fish. They scare easily, and have a mouth like a life saver, because they feed on the bottom. You had to use a pretty small hook to catch them. Andy showed up to help me with his small hook, and I continued using my large hook; in ninety minutes we had twenty-three cusk and three white fish.

There were so many fish we could not carry all of them off the lake. We went back to the fishing shack, and tore some paneling off the bench. The fish were sticky, and they stuck to the paneling. We pulled them ashore like on a sled. We went to Jordan's Store, and laid the fish out on the floor, so Carroll could take pictures for his bulletin board. The excited inquisitive customers asked, "Where did you catch them?"

I replied, "Wards Cove", which was a long ways away from where we had been fishing. The men knew we caught them in a crack from our animated conversation when we arrived.

When we arrived at the lake the next weekend, over twenty men were lined up on the crack leading from Wards Cove.

That spring, as the weather turned warmer, we hauled our fishing shack ashore. The wind was changing direction, and by morning the ice would pull away from the shore.

There were several fish camps on the ice, not far from shore that would be lost to the bottom of the lake by morning. We knew these shacks were private property, and we should not touch them, but we also knew if we could save them, the owners would probably be grateful. We went to the store, and borrowed all the rope we could gather, and returned to pull these shacks onto solid ground. It was a glorious sight to see six shacks standing on terra firma like sentinels, saved by two adventurers.

One Sunday many years later, Buddy was glad for the many times he had watched his dad remove a fishhook. Buddy was the only one at home when a patient rang the doorbell. A man stood there with a fishhook in his arm. Buddy explained Doc was not home. The man said, "You must know how to remove a fishhook."

Buddy replied, "Well, yes, I've removed a few."

The patient s said, "How about helping me out by removing this one?"

Buddy replied, "I can remove the hook, but you need a tetanus shot. My mother would kill me if the hook was removed without a tetanus shot."

The patient said, "I promise I will come in tomorrow for the shot." The man kept his word and Buddy's life was spared.

Log House

When I was in college Dad was working on a big project. He dreamed of building a log house. Neither one of us knew what we were doing, but we talked, and used lots of common sense as we proceeded.

We made a few mistakes along the way. I prefer to call them learning experiences.

The basement had been dug and the concrete foundation walls were up and back-filled when I finished school. Dad and I put the carrying timbers in place, and laid the subfloor, and covered it with tarpaper before winter. The next summer I gathered three boys just out of school to help me, and to keep them out of mischief. We moved the camper to the site so no time was wasted traveling. We laid logs two stories high, and had the roof on before winter. I worked on the inside all winter. The next summer Dad and I put up the stone chimney. After a few years Mom and Dad were able to move into their new log home and Tiffiney and I moved into the house where the office was while I finished building my log home.

Buddy's Log House Porter

When I finished constructing the log house for my folks, I realized I was fascinated with working with logs, and I wanted to learn more about it. I took a job with a man that was doing post and beam construction. I learned how to chisel the mortise and tenon ends of my logs to fit them together for a tight construction. Under my dad's supervision we went to the woods and started cutting down trees, peeling them and piling them in hot yards to dry.

I was able to buy eighteen acres of land on the side of a mountain. The drive up the mountain to the location of the house was nothing more than a skidder trail.

I built a shelter to protect the logs from the snow, and hauled them to the site from Upton. The foundation was poured, and I started laying up the logs. The underneath of each log was scribed, and using the chainsaw the high points were removed. I cut out a vee shaped piece on the bottom of each log. It could carry wires and I put insulation in this space. As I worked I kept inventing new methods of raising the logs, as the walls grew higher to a finished three stories. I put each of the logs in place by myself. Each year I completed one floor. I worked mostly in the winter while I poured concrete in the summer.

I moved the old bread-truck and backed it as close to the house as I could. I chocked the tires so it wouldn't roll. Now, I could come out the basement, open the van, and grab my chisel, wooden mallet, hand auger, and the other tools I used to build the house, and they were safe and not out in the weather. I was still living in Hiram.

I was on my way to my log house on a very cold December day. I saw George cutting down birch trees. He was almost out of firewood. I told him he could come over and take my firewood to get him through the winter. He and his boy made several trips that winter.

Someone stole my Husqvarna chainsaw out of the van. I had locked the back with a key, but he jimmied the sliding door open.

Two years later George's partner stopped me and asked, "Did George ever fess up to you about that saw? You know, his son stole it."

Shortly after that I put a CB in my truck; this was before cell phones, as I was pouring cement all over New England.

I picked up a hitch hiker on Cornish Station Hill. A young, shady-looking juvenile delinquent, but at times, I didn't look that good, either. Don't judge a book by its cover. I dropped him off in Cornish and went about my business.

About a week later Tiffiney and I went to the band concert in Cornish, and when we came back to the truck somebody had slipped the windows open, and stole my AK 47 out of the gun rack, and my four hundred dollar CB radio. I had no idea who it was. It was my own fault for not locking the window. No one should take others people stuff anyway. I found out that not all people are as trustworthy as I am. Now, I am really mad.

George had moved from the Notch Road to Cornish. I had to vent somewhere. I thought this was a good place. I pulled into George's drive and, tooted the horn. When he started to come out, I jumped out of my truck, and I screamed. Every time he tried to say something I screamed more. "My dad took care of you for nothing, I gave you my dry firewood, and then you had the nerve to steal my chainsaw. Don't you ever, ever wave to me again. If you meet me on the road, you better close your eyes, and get out of the way. If you ever wave at me again, I will turn around, and pummel the shit out of you."

I felt better letting him know that I knew what had happened. I never got my chainsaw, gun, or radio back.

I had been building my log house in Porterfield for over two years, and living in the house at Hiram. When the fire burned down the Hiram house. I felt an urgency to get my house ready so we could live there. I decided I could insulate the basement ceiling, put in electricity, and we could move in. I already had a toilet and shower installed in the basement.

It had been snowing for a day and a half. I put the snowplow on the old truck, and drove to Porter to plow out the drive. I made it to the driveway, and I got about half way up the driveway, when I saw smoke coming out of the chimney. That was strange because I didn't even have a stove in the house. I knew something was going on. George and Gene had jimmied the door open and set up an old double barrel stove, one on top of the other for a heat exchange, and brought a cord of firewood with them. They had already put the floor down and the 2x4's studs up for the bedroom walls. They were working on the electricity and plumbing. I knew some of the men and there were others that I did not know, but they were working non-stop.

Carl stopped what he was doing and built the kitchen and bathroom cabinets. Mother sanded and varnished them. I asked a couple men to stop by and give him an estimate for the sheet rock for the inner walls. They took measurements, and went out to their truck to figure out the estimate. They returned and handed it to me. It said, "Zero, zero, zero, zero, if we can do it evenings and weekends."

These men are true friends. Their recreation is not playing golf, but helping those in need. It is too bad that the thieves do not understand this principle.

The town had a white elephant shower for us. We were loaded down with silverware, dishes, pots and pans, and miscellaneous things that neighbors no longer needed.

We slept on the floor on an air mattress for months. Tiffiney cooked on a hot plate, and after eating she loaded the dirty dishes in five gallon buckets, and when she ran out of dishes, she put the pails of dirty dishes in the car, and filled a pillowcase with the dirty clothes, and went to her mother's to do the laundry and wash the dishes. She never complained.

Meanwhile, Bud is busy with his concrete work. He started buying appliances, and hiding them at a neighbor's. First he bought a stove, then a refrigerator, followed by a sink, washer and dryer.

One day Tiffiney had to be gone all day. Helpers came out of the woodwork. They put Formica in the kitchen and the bathroom, others were moving the appliances, and hook them up. There was a big surprise party when Tiffiney came home that night, and to celebrate, she took the hot plate out on the porch, and threw it up in the trees, where it still hangs, as a reminder of days past. She is a great wife!

Life has not always gone smoothly for Bud. Buddy is not one to stand around watching others work.

Furnace

He hired Butch Stacy to put a heating system into the house. Buddy worked alongside him lugging supplies, and doing anything he could to help. By watching, Buddy quickly knew what to do, and he could stay ahead of Butch. Buddy was making level the baseboards, then screwing them in place, sanding the inside and outside of the pipes, putting the flux on them, and toward the end all Butch had to do was run around with the soldering gun, and try to keep up with Buddy. They assembled the entire furnace and manifolds for all the zones in just a few days. Butch was pleased with how quickly Bud picked up, and understood his work, so one day he called him for some help, and Buddy worked with Butch most of that winter, when he wasn't doing concrete work.

One day they were making service calls. Butch knocked on the door repeatedly, but there was no answer; he thought the man might have gone for the mail. Buddy went out back to start shoveling out, so they could take their tools into the basement, and he saw a little hand waving out of the snow. Lying in the deep snow was an elderly man, skinny as a stick, quite tall, and wearing only a light jacket, a pair of loafers, and socks. It was a brutally cold day the man had slipped, and fallen that morning when he was cleaning off the bulkhead, so Butch could get to the furnace in the basement. He always shoveled out for the oilman to deliver. He was nearly frozen, and Butch turned pale white. The door was locked, but Butch unlocked the house by opening the bulkhead door and going in through the basement.

They scooped the man up, carried him inside, and put him on the bed. While Butch called the rescue unit Buddy covered the man with blankets, and then took off the man's wet shoes and socks. Buddy opened the man's shirt, and then his own shirt; he crawled in bed and held the man close using his body heat to warm him.

The EMT crew was impressed with their quick action. Later in that evening one of the men called me, and told me about my son saving this man's life.

They repaired the furnace so the pipes would not freeze, and locked the house. Two days later Buddy stopped at the hospital to check on the old man. Tears ran down his face in appreciation for the quick thinking of his young rescuer. Unfortunately the man had a stroke and died ten days later.

Buddy kept working on his house every spare minute. The following summer he was helping a mason construct the rock chimney two floors high. They were visiting as they worked, and the mason was telling about a young man, twenty-four years old, who was dying of cancer. This young man always wanted the experience of riding a motorcycle, but was too sick now to fulfill this desire. Buddy said, "I have an idea. I have a sidecar on one of my bikes. Do you think we could get him in the side car?"

The excitement grew in these two men as they planned a day that would put *Make a Wish* to shame. That evening they both telephoned all the biker friends they knew, and outlined their plan of gathering, and taking this patient on a biker's trip. Somebody said he would donate a Harley Davidson hat, another a bandana, and the memorabilia grew. Sunday morning Buddy and a few men showed up at the patient's house and lifted the young man into the side car, outfitted him with the biker mementos, and tucked a blanket around his legs. The small assemblage started down the road, and as they passed a gas station twenty-four more bikes fell in behind to form a parade. The sound of the many engines alerted the countryside, and people came out of their houses to wave and cheer. The breeze on the young man's face from riding in the open air dried the tears of joy as they formed, and trickled down his cheeks.

He was exhausted when they returned to his home that evening, but thrilled from the exhilarating trip. He tried to return the Harley Davidson items, but the bikers refused, and told him to hang onto them for the rest of his journey.

Rebuilding Paper Mills

The following is Buddy's description of his job rebuilding paper mills all over the United States.

There was a small depression in 1994; at least all of the residential work had dropped off. I was pouring only a couple floors a week. A welding friend of mine asked me if I wanted to go to Erie, Pennsylvania, for a week to a paper mill shut down. I didn't have anything planned so of course I would go.

There were probably fifty people on this crew, twenty on nights and the rest on days, working twenty-four hours around the clock. My friends Don Kerrigan, part owner of our company, Andrew Faulkner, and I took on this job by ourselves. We worked disassembling a doctor blade from the washer drum tank. This blade is thirty feet by two feet, and one-half inch thick. The factory forms a plate of stainless steel which lays a fraction of an inch off the stationary rolling washer-drum. A tremendous jet of air shoots up under the blade blowing six inches of rinsed compressed pulp off the drum.

I was having a ball; the challenge of this type of work was right down my alley. We used chain falls, cutting torches, and a couple wrenches.

The next week I worked a job in Jay, Maine. They liked my work and I enjoyed the job. Pete Pompeo was superintendent on the night shift. They started me working nights, and once I worked with Pete, he wanted me on his crew. I was on nights until 2000.

In 1995 I worked a few jobs with Trico, but after Wyatt was born, I wanted to be home to spend more time with him. A few years later I bumped into Pete, and he said, "No matter where I go in the country people are always asking about you." I guess I made quite an impression on them, so he asked me if I would come back to work with him. About three years later they asked me to work full time. It means I have to be away from home weeks at a time.

When I first started, we worked as fast as we could on a device, and then worked on the next devise, because we only had enough chain falls to do one job at a time. The other thing was we might muck it up. When we put something back together, it wouldn't turn, and we had to take it apart to figure out what had gone wrong. Now, we are so good at it that we will bid the job for six days, but sometimes we have it done in four days.

The digester is a thermos shaped tank, nine to thirteen stories high, and about twenty feet across, like a big pressure cooker. The men in there are working on floating scaffolding; it goes up and down with electric motors, so they can work at the different elevations.

For the last three years I walk around with a clip board to make sure all parts that are needed are in the right place. Last week I walked six and one half miles in eight hours. They have planners for these jobs to get everything they need, because once we start the job it is too late to have parts flown in. In this pulp mill there are lots of parts. The planner does it once a year and I do it every job. I have now developed a computer program for some mills, and a generic plan for others. It saves writing so much on the clip board. I go in and take a look at what has to be done; I'll go to every devise. I already know what gears, seals, bearings, and type of grease we'll need. I then go to the planner to make sure the parts I need are in stock, or have them ordered immediately.

Chlorine Spill

In 1995 Buddy was working on a job rebuilding a paper mill in Portland, Oregon. This is his description of an accident.

I was working at a paper mill in Oregon. Next to the mill they were unloading a railroad tanker filled with chlorine. They had the wrong hose hooked to it. They had connected a four inch heavy flexible hose to unload the tanker, but it wasn't chlorine acceptable. It was one o'clock in the morning when we realized there was a problem; the chlorine had enveloped the entire area of the train car. My team was the only one caught in it. I had a crew of six men. The fuel welders and fitters were inside the digester with me. I yelled, and we stopped when I smelled the chlorine. We grabbed escape respirators which are a mouth piece like a snorkel with a filter on it, and a little clothespin like thing you put on your nose. We scurried to the opening half way up this thirteen story tank. We escaped out onto a fire escape grating, went across a cat walk, and into an adjacent building, and then down a set of stairs, and out the building. I didn't breathe as I came down, and was out of the chlorine cloud.

When we arrived at the main gate, they turned us upside down at the curbing, because the chlorine is heavy and with your butt up in the air, the chlorine falls, and the air rises above it. As we burped the chlorine came out, and it looked like mountain dew, or yellowish putrid gunk.

I thought I was fine until I was in the ambulance. One of the boys from Buxton didn't have an escape respirator, and he was on the gurney next to me receiving oxygen. Another boy and I, who had escape respirators, were sharing oxygen in the ambulance. I took a breath of the oxygen just to humor the medic while we were on our way to the hospital in Portland, Oregon, and then I gave it to the other boy. That was when I realized how hard it was to breath; I was laboring without fresh oxygen.

We had to take off all our clothes, because they smelled like a bottle of Clorox. They put our clothes in plastic bags, and we wore a jump-suit type garment. They took us to the hospital. I was released after they inspected me. There wasn't anything more they could do for me. They told me it would be difficult to breath for a few days. I caught a ride back to the plant with the rescue unit, and returned to work.

No Power

When we arrived at a job in Kentucky the first thing we did was assemble the floating scaffolding inside the ten story tank, so they could float up and down like window washers. Once it is erected we ride to the top to make sure nothing is going to fall from the top of the tank, and hit anyone. This day my boss and several of the engineers, that run this mill, rode all the way to the top.

Mr. Kerrigan asked me to be the "hole" watch foreman. Whenever anyone is in the tank you have someone there that has communication, a radio or something, so in case something goes wrong, they can get help. They went all the way to the top, and started down when the power shut off. Mr. Kerrigan called on the radio and said, "Buddy, my power is off, check the beakers." It was not uncommon for this to happen. Sometimes when we started spraying inside the beakers will trip.

I called him back and said, "It is not our beaker panel; the mill's power if out." We didn't know why. The mill engineers heard there was an electrical problem up on the hill. They sent someone to check it out.

My boss and the engineers are still stranded high in the tank. It started raining, and I was getting cold. I could see my whole crew sitting in the trailer drinking coffee. These men had worked here forever, and this was only my fourth job that season, but Don had taken to me so much that he wanted me there with him. The men kept coaxing me to join them in the trailer, but I would not leave my place in the hole. There were cables lying in a coil higher than my knee. I stepped over them, and started dragging the cables to the other side and recoiling them. I was doing this to keep warm, knowing I would have to recoil them back where they were. I was concerned about the engineers, hoping they would not panic. I started singing to reassure them they were not alone. On the radio, I hear, "Buddy."

"Yes, Mr. Kerrigan."

"Stop singing, you're no Sinatra." The sound was going into the manway, and up to the top where they were.

Soon we received word that an apprentice electrician had opened a box of very high power. It was allegedly locked out, or had no power to it. When he opened the box, and reached in with his tools, he was electrocuted and killed. They had to take the man down before they could work on the power, but there was no way to lower him without power. Eventually they towed in a portable generator, to supply power to operate the lift, to remove him.

I stayed in the hole until all the men were down and safe.

We make sure everything is safe, and then the mill people come in and do an inspection. They mark with paint the screens they want opened, so we can relay this to our workers after inspection.

The chips are pumped to the top, and the feed unit pushes them down. At the same time fluid is extracted, and recirculated to mix with more chips. These screens take a lot wear and tear, and have to be replaced often.

Trico, Video

I was working on a job I had never done before. I was in a tank shaped something like a funnel. It wasn't a perfect funnel, because one side was steeper than the other. This let the chips fall down through the tank causing the steel to wear thin, on inspection the metallurgists said, "This is too thin, and needs to be replaced with thicker steel." So, instead of building a whole new tank, they brought in precut pieces of steel to patch this funnel, like putting a patch on an inner tube, except these pieces of steel have to be cut so the angles will have the correct slope.

The mill bought the replacement panels the year before, and stacked them in the corner, but they were never labeled. I had to do a little math, the circumference at the top, the circumference on the bottom, the length of the longest piece and then the shortest side. This gave me an idea of where to start. I did all of this in set up. I finally took a crew in there with me. We were probably on the fourth or fifth panel, and several people had been coming by to observe us. I think this was something that worried the mill, and they wanted to make sure everything was going all right. More people came from the main company once they saw it was going well.

I was struggling with a large, heavy sheet of metal. I had to come in through a small window with one welder. When the panels were set in place, and when I was happy with the position he tack welded it in several places, and then he welded the entire piece, and the boys moved on to fit the next piece.

I spotted a man peering down checking things out. He was a very nice gentleman with a round face. I can usually read people just like dogs know if they can trust a man. This helps me to know if I can joke. Well, this project is going so well I didn't have a problem joking. This man stuck his head in, and looked around quite a bit while we were putting up the next few pieces. He called out, "How's it going boys?"

I could tell he was a very pleasant fellow; he didn't have a frown on his forehead. He seemed pleased with our work; I had been watching him out of the corner of my eye.

I said, "It seems to be going pretty good, but if you see us doing something wrong I want you to speak up, because I fell asleep during this part of the video." He looked a little puzzled; I think he thought I was joking, but he thought it was coming out pretty good. He stepped away, and we went back to work, fitting, cutting and welding. I did not realize this was the mill manager. He has the approval of everything in the mill.

He was so impressed to think my boss, Guy, had a video to show us how to clad plate the chipping bin. He went to the trailer and praised Guy for how well he prepared his crews for the job they were doing "You're not like a regular contractor if you research it that much." Guy didn't really understand what he was talking about. He said, "That chip plating is coming out really good, and I think it has a lot to do with the video. That young man down in the pit admitted he fell asleep watching the video."

Guy answered, "Oh, you met Buddy, didn't you?" He described me as wearing a green hard-hat, and everyone else wears red hard-hats.

He replied, "Yes, a very lovely gentleman."

Guy said, "As far as a video goes, we never had a video, but he is a great worker. The biggest reason we keep him around is to entertain us."

Well, that man got such a kick out of my joking with him that he took six other people and me out to lunch after the job was completed.

It helps a lot being a little personable.

Speculum

It was lunch time at the mill, and the men opened their lunch pails. "Hey Bud, what the heck are you doing?" yelled Sam.

Bud replied, "Well, it is lunch time, and I don't want to put my dirty hands on my sandwich! I found this tool in my dad's medical bag." Bud opened the sandwich bag, and carefully grasped his sandwich. He pulled it out of the wrapping without touching the food with his dirty hands,

Sam exclaimed, "Hell, that's a speculum, don't you know what it's used for?"

"Not exactly," Bud replied.

Sam made the darnedest face, squirmed, and snorted, "Hell, Doc sticks that thing into a woman's vagina."

Laughingly Bud answered, "It really works great. I'll let you use it on your sandwich when I am finished."

Sam winced, threw his hands in the air, and yelled, "Get that damn thing out of here!"

Bud knew he had snagged a sucker and he continued, "They come in different sizes. The small one is great for eating grapes." By now Bud had lost his audience, as all of the men had grabbed their lunches, and moved away from this prankster.

Quarters

Buddy has a great wit and many of his practical jokes just happen without his thinking about them, and stuff just pops out of his mouth before he has a chance to polish it. He has learned to be careful when he is representing the company at work.

At work he is one hundred per cent business. If there is room for a little humor that isn't going to hurt anything, he will do it, socially, toward the end of the job. The engineers might have a lobster bake, cookout, or something to show their appreciation, a little PR (public relations). They like Bud because he can talk with all kinds of people.

Buddy relates the following story:

This is one of those things that just happened. I was riding up the freight elevator with about ten people. I reached into my pocket like I was searching for something and said, "Anybody got a quarter?" Usually, three or four guys will hand over a quarter, because they are making $30.00 to $40.00 an hour. This time the only one that offered a quarter was a black guy who was running the lift. He was probably making $5.00 per hour. I said, "Thank you very much, but you keep it." I kept doing this all day wherever I went. I might come up to one of my crews, and tell them they were doing a good job, but watch out for this or that, and just as I am leaving, I'd say, "Do any of you guys have a quarter?" and every time I would get a quarter or two.

At the end of the day I went to the trailer to report to the owner of the company and, Pete my immediate boss, what my three crews had accomplished, where we left off, and the things that needed to be done. They were checking it off on their lists, "Yup, Yup."

As I was finishing I said, "Do any of you have a quarter?" Just as I said this Pete's phone rang, but he heard "a quarter". The owner, Guy said, "Yes, there are three quarters out in my truck, you can have them." I waved him off, just grinning, but not looking, I mouthed "Not you," while Pete was on the phone. Guy is scratching his head wondering what is Buddy up to now? While Pete is still on the phone, he reaches down in his pocket, and comes out with keys and some change. I reached out and took two quarters, and Pete puts the rest back in his pocket. I dropped the quarters into my pocket, and slapped my hand against them so they would jingle.

Guy asked, "What is going on?"

I told him, "I am doing my laundry tonight." Guy couldn't get over that, the best paid kid on his crew was bumming quarters. I told him, "My mom would be some proud of me," and laughed.

A few days later, I was checking out a truck to pick up something at the hardware store. When the clerk looked at my signature, he said, "Oh, you're the 'quarter guy.'"

Questions

The following are questions I asked as I interviewed Buddy:

How did you learn to save or spend money?

Grandpa Cecil Barnes told me when I was really young, "If you don't have the money to buy something, then you don't want it bad enough." He was teaching me not to borrow money to buy something. When you want it bad enough the money will be there. I deduced if I wanted something, I better save for it. This was probably better in his lifetime, because when I was thirty-five-years-old I applied for a credit card and I couldn't get one. I had no credit because I never borrowed for anything. I think this is stupid. They should look at what someone owns with no outstanding liens, and consider him as a good risk.

I was not able to get a credit card, because I didn't exist on paper; I paid cash for everything. I didn't know anything about credit cards. One day I took $4,000.00 cash to a Harley Davidson Dealership to buy a motorcycle that cost $3,999.00. I showed them the money, and explained I was not able to get a credit card, and somebody told me I had to charge something and make payments on time to establish credit.

They knew me at Street Cycles. We often rode together, like the time we took the young man with cancer for a motorcycle ride. They knew me, and they trusted me. I said, "I will give you $2,000.00 and charge the rest, or I will give 25, 30, or 35 hundred, whatever you want so I can establish credit. At that time they were dealing with Ford Motor Company, and they gave me a two thousand dollar loan. I paid it every month. Someone told me it was bad credit if I paid it ahead of time. I paid interest on that one, but I was able to get a credit card. I use a credit card for convenience; I have had it since 1986. I did not pay the full amount once, but it was only once.

Why didn't you cash the checks Grandpa Freese sent you?

"I was making good money". When I was seventeen I worked for $2.70 per hour. I was making my own money, and had plenty for what I needed. Here was a retired couple with God only knows how many grandchildren sending me money. I just burned those checks.

What was your favorite food?

I don't think we had much choice. We never said what we disliked, but learned to ask for a *no thank you helping* to get away with only a teaspoonful. We ate what was on our plate, if we didn't eat it we sat at the table, and then had to work, even if it wasn't your turn.

Do you remember taking dancing lessons with the girls?

THE APPLES UNDER MY TREE

That was just like the band. You took all the younger kids along with the older ones, so I went to ballet and tap dancing lessons. There were times on Saturday mornings you dropped me off at the library, and the librarian, Mrs. Flint, made popcorn for me.

What makes you angry?

The biggest thing I have a problem with is lazy people, people that don't carry their weight. I have zero tolerance, even for my best friends at work, if they don't step up to the plate. I am sure I have offended some, but others have picked up the pace.

Dad used to write big words on the mirror. Do you remember any of the words?

"Oh, heavens no, but I had to know them that week." I remember he taught us to ask for water in Chinese and French.

What are you most proud of?

I think it is my construction of log buildings. The buildings are something no one else has done or showed me. I learned all by myself. I am proud of the round-log work.

Is there anything you wish you had done differently?

He quickly replied, "No"
To which I replied "Good boy"

What was the biggest lie you ever told?

"Oh my, I guess it would be when I was dating. I told the girls not to worry about getting pregnant because when I was a little boy I was on a house call with my dad, and he told me to sit still in the car. I was really little, but I was big enough to open the car door when my dad was out of sight. When I opened the door I fell out into the snow, and I couldn't get up. I laid there in the snow; my little peter was cold and it froze, my nuts froze too, and I can't have babies."

Were you ever bullied?

No, not too much. I didn't hang around with that kind of people.

I do remember one time when our entire family was the bully. It involved a neighbor boy, Jeffery. Any time it was raining in the morning at bus time, Jeffery would leave his house early for the bus stop. He went inside the telephone booth, and closed the door; he shared his space with no one. I wrote the pay-phone number on a note pad, and pinned it to our bulletin board. The next time it rained, I begged my mother to help us. I asked her to call the telephone number when she was sure we had arrived at the bus stop, and somehow get Jeffry out of the phone booth. My mother is a genius. She dialed the number, and when Jeffry answered, she spoke in a stern business like voice, "This is the United States Weather Bureau. I need your help. Would you please step out, hold out your hands, and see how hard it is raining?" When Jeffrey stepped out of the booth the entire neighborhood crammed into the booth leaving him in the rain.

Why are you always busy?

That comes from my parents making sure the children filled their time doing something constructive. All of my brothers and sisters find pleasure in hard work. It is very difficult, if not impossible for them to be idol. Look at my mom in her eighties; she fills every minute writing, and publishing books. Her saying is: "I would rather wear out, than rust out."

What was your most difficult decision?

I was debating whether I should run or stay the day I was married. I was okay with marrying Tiffiney, but I was so nervous standing in the front of the church. All I could think about was everyone was looking at the back of my head. I was anxious to get married and start a family, but just sitting there and waiting was terrible. I would rather have been the bride. I could just walk in after everyone was seated, rather than spending an eternity waiting with everyone looking at me. Dad was my best man ,and I really like Tiffiney's dad.

Margaret's thoughts of the wedding were:

I was in the vestibule of the church when twenty motorcycles roared up and parked in front of the church. I thought, 'Oh My God.' Then, twenty neatly dressed young men walked in quietly, stepped up, and hugged me. And I thought, 'I guess it is all right.'

Buddy told, "The biggest reason we shot red squirrels, was not to kill, but because as rodents, they worked their way into camp. One day we found a bunch of little pink ones under a pillow."

We made our own fun outside. We climbed five or six limbs up in the fir trees, or about twelve feet, and we would hop out on the outside of the branches, and slide all the way to the ground.

What would you do if you won a Million dollars?

I would work with logs. I would build post and beam buildings out of round-wood. I would pour a slab out here; I would cut, peel, and prefab timber frames to ship them out. If someone else did it, it would not be the same.

If you had only one year to live, what would you do?

If I was healthy, I would be on the mountain. I really enjoy that.

What was the best gift you received?

I really liked the red, white, and blue basketball that Debbie gave me. We didn't get a lot of Christmas gifts. The gift you gave us was the gift of work, and to be willing to help others.

What will you tell your grandchildren about your mother and dad?

The same stories I tell everyone else, mostly about work. My son, Wyatt, has a great work ethic, and a lot of that comes from me being the youngest boy. I had to pick up the rake, take care of the shower curtain we dragged the leaves on; I was the grunt. I had two older brothers and I had to do what they said. I was low man on the totem pole. I said if I ever have a boy, he is going to have to pick up the slack like I did.

How did John's death affect you?

I was right at the age where I knew enough. If I had been a little younger, it probably would not have made such an impact. Now, they have grief counselling. I remember the morning of the accident; Harold Douglas' dad picked me up at the orthodontist and took us to Driver's Ed. When the class was over we drove to my house. I saw the band at the Four Corner Store, but I had already decided I could not march that day. I do remember Scotte marched. I went home, climbed the mountain, went out onto the ledges to watch the parade, and I cried.

Who did you look up to?

I appreciated Dan Hester when he taught the math classes after I graduated. The way he taught was not like a high school teacher, but as a college professor. That was a huge help to me in college, because I was taking so many classes. I did not have the pressure on these subjects, and I could devote time to the others.

Percy Lord at Camp Blazing Trail was a great mentor, and my coaches. I guess the biggest was Dad, and the times we went hunting. He taught me how to be quiet walking in the woods, how to read the signs, how to observe the wind, and how to shoot. A lot of my sneaking and chasing I have learned since then, because he didn't have a lot of time for me, and he just put me on a stand. He gave me a tremendous foundation in hunting.

What do you remember about your dad?

I think about him a lot. I was up on the mountain the other day and after I finished chopping, I hooked the last hitch together, and put the saw down. I was trying to find the boundary or a sign. It was slippery; I found a blazed tree, barb wire, and then I found one of the signs. I lined everything up as far as I could see, but there was a lot of foliage. It was kind of hard to follow the boundary line.

When the sun is out, I could orientate myself using the shadows. I lost the boundary and I couldn't find it. In a cursing away at Dad and I said, "Show me a sign or a blaze." I didn't take three steps when I ripped my pants on a piece of barb wire. I said, "Thanks for showing me, but next time don't be so hard on me." I found lots of the stumps where we worked there long ago.

Diane,   Bud   Scotte   Terry
          John   Bill

Front: Doc   Margaret   Terry   Diane

Bud   John   Neil (S. Africa)   Scotte

Scotte

    Scotte was an adorable rosy-cheeked baby with three older brothers, six-year-old Bill, three-year-old John, and one-year-old Buddy. I did not think my chances of having a girl were very good, so I only picked out the name Scott. When I saw this lovely robust baby, I knew she could take care of herself if anybody teased her about her name.

    I now had two babies in diapers; Buddy was not walking yet. My hands were full with four little ones, a household to manage, and an office to keep fit and running. I was barely twenty-five, and too young to be thought of as "THE DOCTOR'S WIFE."

    I finally had a girl to sew for, but she was almost two years old before I had time to sew. I had no time to shop for material, and very little money, so I took a pair of old floral drapes, and made a princess formal for a Christmas gift. She loved that dress; every morning after she was dressed I put the formal on over her clothes. Several years later I made the three girls chiffon gowns with matching slips, and made matching dresses for their dolls. I hand-washed the thin formals every night, and they dried overnight, ready to be worn the next day.

    She had a motherly instinct as a small child, and she cared for her sisters, patient's small children, and spent hours with her baby dolls.

    One Saturday evening at Upton, Scotte was curled up in my arms as the rocking chair gently moved rhythmically. I asked, "What do you think Daddy is doing?" Her response tickled me.

    She dreamily replied, "He has patients, and he is rubbing them forth and back, forth and back."

By the time she was four years old, she was baking brownies every morning. I laid out the ingredients, and she learned how to use the oven, measure the ingredients, break the egg, and mix the brownies. Her brothers needed no lessons on how to eat them.

Dad often brought home young wild animals. This time it was a baby porcupine. We repeatedly told the small children they should not pet the adorable little ball, because of his prickly quills. Scotte was determined she was going to mother this little orphan. She disappeared into the house, and returned wearing her dad's lead lined x-ray gloves.

The children played outdoors a lot, because if they were in the house they had to work. Neighborhood kids were part of their fun and games, not to mention disagreements. Susan as the oldest was delegated to be the teacher for their self-organized school. They planned class trips in the neighborhood where they learned how their ancestors lived, how to run a business, read Longfellow's poems, and then visited his grandmother's home. They visited her cemetery, and ate their bag lunches there.

Scotte took group ski lessons when she was in the second grade. She wasn't very brave, and never went beyond the Bunny Hill. Her checks were always rosy red; every time she came down the slope, with her jacket unzipped, they thought she was cold, and zipped her jacket to her chin.

I asked, "Did the whistle I used, to call you in from play, upset you?"

I didn't mind the whistle; it was a good thing. If you wanted only one child, you waved the others back to their activities, and none of us wanted to miss a meal.

What did I do that upset you the most?

I don't think there were too many things that upset me, because I do the same things myself as a mother.

THE APPLES UNDER MY TREE

I asked Scotte to tell me about some of her early memories.

We had a long-playing record of children's songs that we played after breakfast. We danced, and sang to it while mother did dishes, and cleaned the kitchen. I liked the way Daddy came through the room when we had our record on; he did a funny little dance, and the change in his pocket jingled. We all loved *Splish splalsh I was taking a bath*, and Buddy did a funny dance to that song.

Daddy took me to nursery school, and I often went on house calls with him. It was very cold in the winter, and the heater didn't work very well in the Volkswagen. I put my fingers next to the defroster to warm them, and then put them on Daddy's neck and face. He exclaimed, "Oh that feels so good!" Then I did it again. He used to sing to me as we drove down the deserted county roads.

I sat on the edge of the front seat of the Volkswagen, holding the handle near the windshield, bouncing to the rhythm of the music, and my pony tail swishing from side to side. I almost wore out the seat.

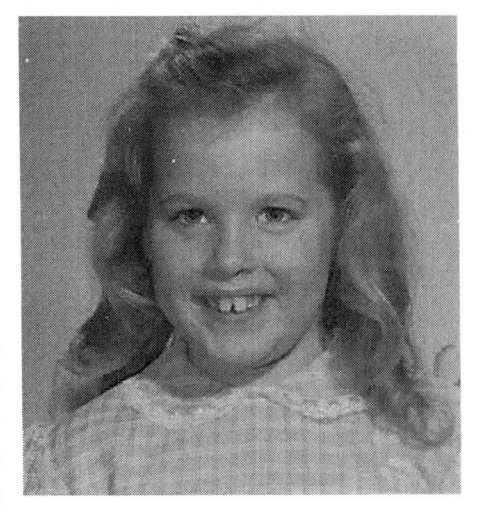

Mr. Cotton's Store was a fascinating place. I liked watching him slice bologna, and making hamburg. He put on a white apron splotched with dried blood, a white paper hat like a soldier's hat, and then washed his hands before he stepped into the cooler. I peeked in and saw half a cow hanging inside. When he made hamburg he brought the metal parts of the grinder from the cooler, and attached them to the motor. Then he went back into the cooler, and brought out a huge chunk of meat, and laid it on the table. He picked up his knife, and sharpened it on his steel, before he cut the meat into little pieces. He was very good at judging how much meat he needed to make two pounds of hamburg. I watched him poke the small pieces of meat into the grinder, and saw the hamburg squirt out and fall on the paper, and then he ground the hamburg again.

A big wheel of sharp cheese, covered with cheesecloth to keep off the flies, sat near the counter. Sometimes he sliced off a small piece, and gave it to me. One day he took the lid off a barrel that stood in the middle of the store. I looked in, and it was gross. I made a face, and he told me it was pickled tripe, or the lining of a cow's stomach. The other barrel held very large pickles.

My mother was a good teacher. At an early age she taught me to cook and bake. We started helping with the meals, and doing dishes when we were very young. The neat thing was she worked next to us, and made it fun. She moved the sewing machine to the kitchen, so if we were baking, she was sewing, but always available if we needed help. Likewise, if we were sewing, she was cooking, not hovering over our every stitch. If we made a mistake in our sewing she helped us rip it out, and then sewed what had been ripped out, so we could proceed. We didn't feel defeated by our mistake, but looked at it as a learning experience.

There was not a 4-H Club to encourage us with projects, so she started one for the entire community, and worked this into her busy schedule.

This is a story Scotte often tells about one of the last surgeries she observed.

I was working on my 4-H project; Mother was busy when I was ready to sew the hem. I thought I could do it by myself. Painstakingly, I sewed all the way around the entire skirt by hand, and then I realized I had done it on the wrong side. I tried to take out the tiny stitches, but it made holes in my skirt, and I knew I had to start from scratch.

I was trying to forget about my bad sewing job, and I went to see what Daddy was doing in the surgical room. Instinctively, I put my hands behind my back, as I had been taught, whenever I entered this room.

Dad had a man lying on the surgical table with chain saw cuts on his arm, and he was patiently closing the many cuts. Dad asked me if I wanted to do the stitching, and I said, "Oh no, you would have to tear out my stitches."

Scotte continues:

Mother told us we could win money by entering projects at the fair. She showed us the list of the categories, and the prize money awarded for each. We decided to make doughnuts. There were two groups, plain and chocolate. Mother took the rules seriously, and she would not allow us to make only one batch of each kind, so each of us could pick out three doughnuts for our entry. Oh no! We each had to make our own batch. That meant six batches all together. Dad and the boys gladly volunteered to eat the doughnuts, and Mother put many of them in the freezer. The kitchen floor was covered with a dusting of flour, and dozens of doughnuts sat in pans on the table and counter.

Those were only two of our entries. Mother, who had never made a Christmas wreath in her life, was going to show us how to create a winning masterpiece. While I was making my doughnuts my sisters headed for the mountain with pruning shears and basket to cut fir boughs.

I was frying my doughnuts, Diane was mixing her batter, and Terry was cutting the fir boughs into small sprigs of evergreen. You had to be careful walking in the kitchen, because the floor was slippery from the fir needles and flour.

Mother labeled, wrapped the six plates of doughnuts, and carried them to the car while I carried the four scrappy looking wreaths, hoping they would hold together until after judging. Mother also entered four jars of canned meat and fish.

All of us were awarded ribbons, and money for our food, and right after judging we placed our wreaths deep in the trash can.

Music

Scotte was musically and artistically talented. She started playing the clarinet and organ when she was in the third grade, and she was in the band by fifth grade. She never needed to be reminded to practice. Mr. Fuchs' lessons gave her a great start, and they were only two dollars.

When the children were older and busier they did not want to practice, but the teacher and I wanted them to continue playing, so we bought quartet music for each instrument. They did not have to practice during the week, but on lesson day the four of them sat, and played for an hour. They were also called upon to play after Thanksgiving and Christmas dinner when we invited four elderly people to join us for the day.

When Scotte was ten years old the family attended a home show in Portland, and a huge man was demonstrating a Conn Organ. She asked him if she could play and he said, "Get away little girl." She stood back quietly, and watched him. Pretty soon a crowd gathered around the organ, and he slid off the bench to make his pitch, and hopefully a sale. When the bench was empty Scotte slid onto it, and started playing, "Yellow Bird".

He started shutting down all the tabs to eliminate the sound. The people were intrigued with this little girl, and soon he started lifting the tabs.

Scotte found she could avoid many of her chores if she slipped away, and played the organ. We enjoyed the music so much that we did not get after her about her tasks. She taught herself to play piano. If there was a pot luck supper, and it was time to clear the tables, Scotte went to the piano, and started playing while the others cleared the tables.

The evening patients were subjected to unimaginable sounds. John was blasting songs from Herb Alpert and the Tijuana Brass Group on his trumpet. The other instruments were squeaking and squawking while Scotte was playing the organ. One day a blind man heard the organ music, he enjoyed it so much he bought an organ, and learned to play.

Many years later Scotte spent her evenings playing the organ at Stone Ridge Restaurant where her brother and sister worked. I returned to the sewing machine, and made several evening gowns for her.

There were two children that did not participate in music. Bill would rather tear motors apart, and build race cars. Terry, the youngest pleaded, "No music, please. I will run every event in track, and do all the other sports, but no music."

Family

I asked Scotte to tell me about memories of her grandparents.

Grandpa Freese spent Christmas with us when I was two-years-old. I was sitting on his lap, and he lit a cigarette. I did not like that, and I squirmed to get down. Finally, he realized it was the tobacco smoke. Holding me was more important to him than the cigarette, and he vowed to never smoke another cigarette the rest of his life.

When I was little I grabbed ahold of his thumbs, and tried to run up his legs; then he flipped me over. When we visited them in Ohio, he took us for rides in his little, red wagon. I enjoyed watching the train behind their house as it went back and forth picking up freight cars. We went to the Mall once, and he bought each of us a helium filled balloon. I remember walking, proudly, down the mall with it tied around my wrist. When we arrived home one of the boys lost their balloon in a tree. It was quite an adventure trying to reach it.

On one trip Mother took us to a fire station, a dairy, a place where they printed the newspaper, a shop where they made candles out of bee's wax, and to the Ohio Caverns. She was always teaching us something new.

Scotte continues, when I took my children to Ohio Grandpa gave them the same experiences he gave me. He showed my girls the marbles in the garden, the bunnies, and gave them a ride in the wagon.

When we were older we took turns sitting behind Grandpa on his big motorcycle as he gave us rides. (Scotte is now crying in the interview.) We rode to Rattlesnake Pond, or to the Bull Ring watering tub. I remember being in Upton, ready for bed, when we heard the motorcycle, and saw the lights of the motorcycle coming up the hill. Everyone ran outside. I loved my Grandpa Freese.

Grandma Freese spent a lot of time in the kitchen, and I sensed she didn't want a bunch kids around when she was cooking. She was better when we were older, or maybe I should say we behaved better when we were older. She had a candy jar and a cookie jar in the kitchen cupboard. I snuck into the kitchen and, grabbed a cookie, and then I went outside, or sat on the back stairs to eat it. Grandpa was there when we were young and rambunctious; he kept us busy and out of her hair.

Grandpa Barnes used to call me skinny, and I called him fat-so, because we were just the opposite. He had a baldhead. Grandma used to make oatmeal cookies with ground-up raisins in them. The raisins made little brown specks in the cookies. Grandpa had spots all over his hands and arms. I thought the spots were from the cookies.

He used to give us a quarter for the Sunday newspaper. All of us competed to bring him the paper, and grab the quarter. We ran to the car the minute we saw him in the drive.

I remember one time when I was at nursery school, playing outside, and I saw them drive by. They had just returned from Florida; I wanted to go home to see them. I never saw him too rough or gruff. If he was, I just backed off. He was a jokester. When he talked he used bad words, not mean or angry, it was just the way he talked. I don't think he even knew he was using cuss words.

I remember when I was five years old we were at a birthday party at Rattlesnake Pond for Dennis, our neighbor, and somebody came and brought us home. They told us Grandpa had died. We went home, and had to be very quiet, because Grandma and all of us were sad.

Grandma Barnes was always humming. She told me she started doing it when Grandpa had his heart attack, so he could tell where she was.

Oh! I remember her peanut butter sandwiches with homemade raspberry jam; they were the best. My eyes opened wide as I watched in great anticipation when she used a wide spatula to spread the peanut butter right to the edges, and then she careful spread the jam on top the peanut butter.

She was so pretty with her dark twinkling eyes, rosy cheeks, and a colorful, bright scarf holding her hair neatly in place. I spent the night once, and when she got up in the morning I saw her unkempt long hair hanging down over her nightie; it was a frightening sight for a little girl. She dried her hair by the kerosene stove after it was shampooed.

I went for a walk in the woods near her house, and a yellow jacket stung me. I ran for the house, and up the porch. Grandma wrapped an afghan around me, and held me, and then she put baking soda and ice on the sting.

I asked Scotte to tell me about memories of her siblings.

Neil was a handsome exchange student from South Africa; he lived with us for a year. I was at an age where I was just noticing boys; he handled it so well. I am sure he knew I was infatuated with him, but he spent time with me as a brother, and he fit right in with our family.

The rules were lightened as each child came along. Billy could never use the car even though he had his driver's license. I did not think it was fair the way Dad treated him. Dad blamed him for anything that went wrong. Bill had to put up with heavy duty thumbs down as he was often told, "No you can't."

John was my protector when I was younger, but he upset me when he called me fat-so. He had the station wagon, and took us swimming and other places, and then all was forgiven.

It was difficult on all of us when John was killed in the automobile accident. I was fourteen when he died; I worked hard to help Daddy build the memorial porch at Upton. It was nice having time with my dad. He usually said things in a positive way, and made me feel good about myself.

I drove the Blue Dream and the Jeep to gather rocks for the porch, and then I started mixing the cement for Dad. I was bummed that I was not there the day the floor was poured, so I did not get to write my name in the wet concrete.

Buddy and I got along very well. I felt sorry for him when he was put back in the fourth grade with me. I took him under my wing and said, "Come on Buddy we are going to do this together." He is a good character.

One winter day in the fifth grade, I was standing on a snow bank with the basketball hoop behind me. A boy came up behind the backboard, and he was looking up my dress. Buddy saw him doing this; he went over, and beat him up, yelling, "Don't you ever look up my sister's dress!" From that day on I really admired Buddy, because he was my protector, and was there for me.

My sister, Diane, is very different from me. There are times she is great, and I love her so much, and other times we are at each other. When we were growing up I pretty much kept my distance from Diane. I felt my youngest sister, Terry, needed to be protected from Diane, so I was in the middle trying to stop their fighting. Finally, I learned to avoid her. It was much better when I had my own bedroom on the third floor.

Terry was my baby sister, and I mothered her, and took care of her.

Each of us moved forward in our individual activities, and with our own friends.

We wore mostly dresses to school. Mother sewed beautiful dresses for us, and shorts with tops for our summer play clothes. We didn't have many pants except snow pants. We all had long hair pulled back in a ponytail. Sometimes I had two ponytails. We curled our hair every night so it wouldn't be tangled with snarls in the morning.

We were taught to conserve water which meant three girls in the tub together. We went downstairs, turned our head upside down over the register to dry our hair, then put our hair in curlers, and off to bed.

Jobs

My first job was when I was about eight years old, babysitting for Barbara, taking care of three little girls. The first time she brought them to our house, and later I stayed with her at her house at Two Trails. She was home, but was busy taking care of customers, and my job was to keep the kids out of her hair. Before that I worked shoveling snow, and picking blueberries. It took a long time to pick a quart of blueberries, but we made a game of it, and Mother helped. I just kept thinking of the blueberry cakes and pies she baked every day.

We did not get an allowance, but we were paid if we did a job beyond our daily tasks.

Dad volunteered my young body to weed the flower gardens for Lydia, one of his elderly patients. I gladly handed this job down to my younger sisters after a couple years.

I had been weeding for a long time one day. There were bushes along the wall of the garage, and I saw a nest of baby birds. I stayed away from the nest, and went to my left pulling weeds. I saw a snake heading toward the birds. I picked him up, he wrapped around my arm, and that frightened me. I never had a snake do that to me, so I threw him down. The snake went back toward the baby birds, and I said, "No you can't touch the birds." I picked him up again, and he bit me through my rubber glove. Two of his fangs hit my fingernail, but one bit me on the underside. I threw him down again, stepped on his tail, and then I grabbed him near the top of his head. He opened his mouth 180 degrees. I threw him across the road as hard as I could. Probably, the best throw I ever made. He landed in the trees somewhere. When I returned to the birds they were gone. I watched the mother bird flying back and forth.

I went to church camp when I was nine, but I didn't get homesick, because I had been away from home on my baby sitting job. I also worked pulling weeds for Rose Wilkinson. She came out, and put a shirt over my back. I didn't realize how badly burned I was getting; it was a really bad burn.

My next job was taking care of Percy's little boy, Jon. He was born with a cardiac defect, and was frail. Percy was the caretaker and assistant to the Lyn, the administrator of Camp Blazing Trail, a girl's camp where my brothers worked. I lived with Jon's family; my duties were to dress him when he woke up, and telephone for a car to take us to the junior camp. I helped Granny fix our breakfast. After we ate, my job was to keep an eye on Jon, and play with him. It was a neat job, because I was able to see my brothers, and it didn't seem like work. Toward the end of the summer Lyn gave me a scholarship to be a camper for two weeks. I lived at the camp, and joined in the many camp activities. Lyn said this was a reward for being such a good babysitter.

I took over the job of cook's helper when Buddy left Blazing Trail. I worked with Granny for three summers. I was looking for a job when I was in college. I observed the freshman kids washing dishes, and sorting silverware. I was not interested in those menial tasks. When I made out my application, I noted that I worked three years as a cook's helper, and I got the job working with the chef.

I worked at the Fryeburg Nursery with my sisters on April vacation. That was my first big paying, hardworking job, and I learned where a dollar came from. The first day was scary, surrounded by dirty-looking old men. I was glad my sisters and a couple neighbor boys were with me.

One summer I cleaned cottages for Jordan Reality with Erica, and when I had my driver's license my sisters, Terry and Diane, worked with me.

I was a night person, and liked to sleep late in the mornings. Mother found me a job as a waitress in a small diner for the early morning shift. This changed my whole life, and I soon learned I could get much more done in a day if I was up early. Mother made me three smocks with pockets to hold my tips. One smock was a loud floral print, and I grumbled about wearing it. Mother said, "I want you to wear it the next rainy morning, and keep your usual smile on your face. Your tips will be higher, because your brightly colored smock and cheerful smile will bring them joy on that dismal day. She was right.

The owner was a man that liked to grope his waitresses. An older lady ran interference for me, and taught me how to handle such people.

For your information: Reece's Peanut Butter Cups were five cents. I must have purchased several of these for this bit of information to reside in my memory.

I had many jobs through my teens. One thing for sure, I was never idle.

As a child I hated picking blueberries until the check came in. I remember getting a check for ten dollars. I went straight to the bank, and then I had to figure out what a signature was. They let me just print my name. When I was older it was a pleasure to pick blueberries. A bunch of us from Blazing Trail went to Upton and picked blueberries. At six o'clock the next morning three of us sat in a canoe, and paddled around the pond. One girl had a bell. Ding, ding, ding and we called out, "Blueberries, blueberries." The people were getting up, and some were getting their boat ready for a day of fishing. We sold quite a few quarts, and then we turned around, and paddled like crazy to get back in time for work.

Many years later I had an appointment at 11:45 a.m. for an interview for a teaching position. I figured the committee would be starved by that time, so I took a box of cookies. I don't know if it helped me get the job, but many of them never forgot the gesture.

All of us, except Billy, had to spend years with the orthodontist. The thing I hated the most about the orthodontist was putting on the bands. He put on the band, and then took his instrument to pull it back so it snapped in place. That was the worst thing. They don't do this anymore, and I was bummed that my children did not have to go through that. Braces were a good thing, and we managed to survive.

Buddy lost two retainers, usually by wrapping them in a napkin at school, and then throwing them in the trash. He tied a clip to a piece of rawhide, and wore it like a necklace. At lunch he removed his retainer, and clipped it to his necklace. Some of the kids freaked out, but he lost no more retainers.

Switzerland

When I was in the eighth grade Uncle Jack took a group of kids from Bonney Eagle to Switzerland. He had room for three more students, so he took his son Brooke, one of Brooke's classmates, and me on the trip. The mountains were spectacular, like nothing I had ever seen. On a glorious, sunny, summer day the group signed up at the base of the mountain to take a long hike in the Alps. We started climbing, and climbing.

There were many switch-backs as we went through the woods. We rested at a park area near the top, and I lay down a little longer than everyone else. I heard them leave, but I just needed to rest a little bit longer. I could not see anyone when I stood up, and looked around. I walked to the left, and I saw the town where we started and the train. I walked some more, and now the town was off to my right; I saw the whole village. I figured I better concentrate on the direction I was taking. When I arrived at the village I decided I needed an ice cream cone to soothe my nerves. I paid for the ice cream, and as I turned to leave, Cousin Brooke came in. He scolded me for not keeping up with the group. Now everyone was together, and we hiked further to a village in the Alps. It was different than the villages in the valley. The buildings were different, and there was farmland. We walked part way on a dirt road.

Jack told Brooke where he wanted to go, and what he wanted to see. The group split into two teams. Brooke led the more able-bodied kids, and Jack took the others up an easier route. When we arrived at the highlands I saw a house, and imagined it was Heidi's. I am sure I started to sing the songs from, *The Sound of Music*. I was dancing, spinning around, and falling in the field. From there we kept going until we found a trail. It wasn't even a path. I just remember trudging through the woods, but Brooke seemed to know where he was going.

We found the castle, or rather a stone structure that was in ruins, which Jack told us to watch for. The woods had grown up around it. Part of it was still standing. We walked around and tried to visualize a magnificent castle from the rubble of this stone edifice. After our imaginations were filled we went back down the mountain. Brooke did a good job leading us to Jack and his group.

Memories of a Small Child

Mother asked John and me to take Dad's medicine to him. I was four and John was seven. We heard a chain saw off in the distance, and we followed the sound. We came to a man and asked if he had seen Dr. Barnes. He told us he had not and John asked, "Where are we?"

He replied, "You're in New Hampshire. Are you kids lost?"

John said, "No" and I stood behind him saying we are too. He tried to quiet me as we turned around and headed back, but I kept thinking, we are lost, yes we are.

We came to a clearing where there was lots of wood piled up. John said he knew where he was, and then we heard the horn which I thought was a moose. John said, "No, Dad is on the porch blowing the horn." I heard footsteps, and I knew it was a moose. John said, "No, that is Mom coming to get us."

I said, "It's a moose!"

"Well, if it's a moose what are you going to do? Do you think you can climb that wood pile?" I knew there was no way I could climb that pile of wood, but I figured fear and adrenaline would get me up on the pile of wood. I was pretty shaken up. Pretty soon we saw Mother walking down the path carrying a smaller cow horn.

We went ice fishing with Dad when we were little, but he didn't have time after he started building the house at Upton. Mother and Dad worked all the time on the house, and we made our fun and games in the woods. We arrived Saturday afternoon just in time to watch the *Adams Family* while mother fixed supper.

Dad was trying to train his new dog, Judy, to chase bobcats. He set a trap to catch a bobcat, so his dog could get the smell of the prey. All of us kids were watching the trapped cat, and I was afraid the cat was going to get out of the trap and get me, but seven-year-old Buddy held out his arms to protect me.

Dad found some porcupine in a tree, and he took all of us kids hunting. He let me try first. He handed me the shotgun, and I aimed into the tree, but I didn't have the gun against my shoulder tight enough, and it kicked back, and hit me in the nose. Dad gave me the empty shell, and I put it in my right pocket. Then he gave Bill the shot gun, and he shot the porcupine. It fell out of the tree, and when he ejected the shell I picked it up, and put it in the left pocket. I had my souvenirs, and Bill collected the bounty for the porcupine.

A man who lived down the road stopped in front of the house where patient's cars were parked. All of us ran toward him, and he put a dime in each of our hands. Daddy saw this from the window. I came dancing through the yard so pleased I had a dime. Dad came roaring out the back door, grabbed ahold of me, and hit me with his belt. He hit me again and again, yelling, "Don't ever take money. Don't ever take money." He kept hitting me, and I wet my pants. I never understood why he gave me such a beating, or why he felt I did something wrong. He never explained why, and I never understood why until I had children of my own. Never take money from a man.

Every kid in town was lucky to have free swimming lessons. That was neat because no one was left sitting on shore while the others had fun. Most of us had our life saving certificate before we were fourteen. As a little girl I looked up to the older girls.
Last week we had a chilly morning, and it reminded me of swimming lessons at Burnt Meadow Pond, and the cold water.

Clarence

Clarence Douglas was a very gentle man, and a special friend. I was nine years old when I went with Dad on a house call, and I saw the animals. I loved animals; Clarence said I could come back any time.

Dad taught me how to ride a bicycle, and I rode up to Clarence's, because he had animals. I felt lonesome like an only child even though I wasn't, so I frequented his place when I wasn't busy babysitting.

I wanted a pet pig so badly. I tried to find a place where I could keep a pig, but Mother was adamant that a pig was not a pet, so I went to Clarence's, and helped him take care of "OUR" animals.

He taught me about the feed he gave the cows, and showed me how to milk Bessie. He had several other cows and calves. The little calves had very rough tongues. I squirted some milk on my sweatshirt, and held my shirt out tightly. The calf's very long tongue came out, and licked the milk off my shirt.

Clarence showed me the different grains he used for their feed. One morning he pulled out a handful of grain and said, "Smell it, Scotte. What do you smell?"

"Molasses?"

"Yup, that's a special treat for those critters."

The big old sow finally had her piglets, and he explained to me not to go near her when she had babies. I calmly backed out to let her know I meant no harm. When the piglets grew bigger, I claimed one as mine and named it Pig.

I mucked out the pig pen, and behind the cows.

He had sheep in the pasture with their little ones, and chickens and ducks hunting for bugs in the yard.

He told me to never bring boys to the farm. I probably wanted to ask why, but I didn't. One day I broke my promise; my brother, Buddy, went with me. I thought it was okay because he was my brother. Clarence was not home. I went into the barn to check on the farm animals, and did my usual routine. I came out, and Buddy was out in the pasture, riding one of the sheep, like a bucking bronco. I am watching him break the rules, and then I realized why Clarence asked me to never bring any boys. I never went back to Clarence's after that, because I had broken my promise.

Newfoundland

I have many memories of our visits to Newfoundland as children. The wind was blowing hard the afternoon we climbed to the top of the highlands. We were wearing lightweight windbreaker jackets, and the wind filled our jackets with air. We looked like balloons being tossed in the wind. After we climbed to the top we lay down, and rolled down the pasture. This was something we did at home in Tuft's field.

When we were older you showed us movies of that day, and we saw ourselves and how funny we looked. I remember looking over the cliff into the ocean, and seeing dead carcasses at the base of the cliff, and there were a couple dead sheep in the pasture. In the distance there was the tinkling of a bell, and then we saw the flock of sheep in an adjoining pasture.

We saw cows wandering down the road; the people had fences around their houses, and they shut the gates to keep the cow out. The cows had free range, but they seemed to find their way home each evening.

I remember Grace's homemade bread; one slice covered a dinner plate. For breakfast she treated us to a slice of her bread spread with a caramel spread we could only buy in Newfoundland. We made sure Mom bought some to bring home.

We swam in a brook that led to the ocean, and watched the men build the log cabin, so we had a place to stay when we returned. In the evening Grace's kids took us to the Honky Tonk, where we hung out with them, and their friends.

Thoughts

Mother tried to convince me I was the answer to her problem. She explained, "Scotte, you are a leader. I think you should start a new trend. You see, every family has a box of socks with no mates. These socks are good, and do not have holes in the toe. It is up to you to convince your peers it is cool to wear socks that don't match." I was a bit hesitant to take this drastic step. I proceeded with baby steps. I was dressing for a basketball game, and I put on one white sock with red stripes, and the other foot I wore a white sock with blue stripes.

I stepped onto the basketball court to warm-up, before the game, and the coach called me over, and told me to go change my socks. I told him, "My mother told me to wear these socks; I don't have any others." He let me play, but as a leader, I was not able to convert many followers.

I have another story about team uniforms. Kezar Falls had a building where the kids played games of pick-up basketball. I was there one Saturday, and timidly asked if I could play. The big "jock" said, "Sure, but you have to be on the skin's team." I left the room blushing. I thought about my defeat all week, and the next week I went prepared to take on my adversary. Again, I asked if I could play, and again he said, "Sure, but you have to be on the skin's team." I crossed my arms in front of me, and reached for the bottom of my T-shirt to pull it over my head. Now, he was the one quivering in retreat. He did not know I was wearing two T-shirts.

Did you have any idols growing up?

My first idol was my mom because she taught me how to take care of the baby, cook, and do ironing. I aspired to be like her. I recall Aunt Donna was living with us. I wanted to talk and act like her. When I was a teenager, and first heard the word idol, I realized I never really had an idol like the Beetles, or the Monkeys. This was not my culture or interest. There were no groups or anybody I connected with, or that inspired me.

I was in the seventh grade when we went to Billy's graduation. There was a girl, Connie Kendall, in that graduating class. She received a silver bowl with her name engraved on it. It was given to her for being involved all four years in sports, music, maintaining excellent grades, and the most difficult part was being highly involved in extracurricular activities. I wanted that bowl! She motivated me more than anyone else, even though I never met her. That was my goal all through high school. I made it; I received my silver bowl with my name engraved on it when I graduated. I was then the inspiration for both of my sisters, and they each have their own silver bowl.

Many years later both Connie and I came back to SAD 55 to teach. I was involved with several other teachers working on the health curriculum. A group of us went to Augusta for a conference. Connie was in my Volkswagen, and we ate together that day. I told Connie something she never knew. I told her how much she had inspired me.

Are there any other stories I have never heard?

I never told you this story, but one year a bunch of us girls went to the log cabin on the mountain in Hiram We arrived just before dark; we built a fire in the stove, and lit the lanterns. There was a loft with a mattress on the floor, and bunks were around the wall of the room. I am afraid of heights, but I remember getting up into the loft. It took a long time to gather enough courage to make the climb. I am lying on the mattress in the loft looking down at the others.

My red-headed friend was older than any of us. She was starting to come of age. Somebody wanted to know if she had red hair in her privates. She didn't want to share that information with us. The girls started chasing her around the cabin trying to catch her to pull her pants down. Through all the commotion one of the lanterns was tipped over, and we had a fire. I was in the loft, and they were screaming FIRE, FIRE. I was scared to pieces, and thought this was where my life was going to end. The girls managed to put out the fire, and I finally climbed down. We walked off the mountain that night, as all of us were too scared to stay. I don't think "Red" hung around with us much after that.

The following is a story Scotte told me:

Learning to drive was easy because we had the Blue Dream. (The Blue Dream commonly called the doodlebug was a homemade vehicle using an Austin frame, a Briggs & Stratton engine, and a homemade truck bed.) We drove it all over the fields of Upton.

Learning how to use the clutch was a little more difficult, especially on a hill. You were letting me drive your car down Hansen Road, a back road, to learn how to drive on the hills. You coached, "You should let up on the gas just before you reach the top of the hill." I was practicing that and doing quite well, when you told me I needed to speed up, saying, "I'd like to get there today, dear."

I was working at Blazing Trail in Denmark the summer I had Driver's Ed. Mr. Demers was my instructor; he picked me up at Camp, and then took me back when I was finished.

I was driving down a country road, and a couple dogs ran across the road in front of me; I didn't bother to brake for them. I figured, get out of the way or die. Mr. Demers didn't believe that was the correct attitude. He had to use his brake.

Pet Pigs

I finally had my pig when I was an adult, and could make my own decisions. Suzie and Sally were mine. That fall I refused to let them kill the pigs for food, and we kept them over the winter. We thought if they had piglets maybe we could recoup some of the money spent on the food they ate over the winter. They were too big, now, to be good eating.

We took Suzie and Sal to Sebago where a man had a boar. Suzie was impregnated, but Sal never had any babies. Suzie had eight piglets, and Sal was the great-aunt. We were able to sell all the piglets when they were bigger, except for the one male that I kept; I named him Chester.

Chester was the name my husband wanted for a boy. I didn't want the name Chester, because I grew up with a Chester. It was not that I did not like him, but he scared me. I was hoping if we had a boy my husband would not want to name him after a pig. Our son was named after my great grandpa and Bruce's uncle. Fortunately, he let go of the name, Chester.

Chester proved to be a good little boar. We ended up selling Chester, but we never recovered all the money we put into food for Suzie and Sal.

When the piglets were small, they could go under the electric fence, but Aunt Sally did not like having them outside the fence where she couldn't control them. It was her position in the family to tend the children. Her charges were on the wrong side of the fence, so Aunt Sal just charged through the fence to be with her nieces and nephews. When she was free in the yard she found locations where the sun shined down on her. She located a piece of black plastic near the garage that collected the warmth of the sun. This was her heavenly place to slumber. She stretched out, and you could see the joy on her face. Happy Girl!

Sal was still free ranging after the piglets grew up and were sold.

I heard a knock at my door. It was a mother and two daughters, of a certain religious sect, knocking while the father and boys sat in the car. Big, old Sal came thundering around the corner, and tried to climb the steps, pushing the visitors aside. Terrified, they ran to their car, slammed the doors, and kicked up clouds of gravel as they hurriedly departed. I am yelling after them, "She just wants to be loved."

The pigs managed to get out of their fenced in area several times when Mom and Dad were babysitting my kids, and they had to chase after the pigs to bring them home.

They had to deal with Scotte's pigs, that she never had as a child. I yelled at Dad one time when we were herding them home. He struck my pig across her back with a branch. I yelled, "Don't you ever hit my pig, Mister!" Yelling at my dad was something I never thought of doing. It broke my heart after I did it, and I felt badly.

He said, "Don't let them get free again." I had to call, and apologize a few days later for yelling at him.

I enjoyed my pet pigs, Susie and Sal, and it was difficult to let them go.

Building House

Bruce and I were building our house, one box of nails at a time. Mother had an old refrigerator in her basement where we kept our perishables. Every morning I put the food I wanted for the day in my insulated ice chest. It was a blessing when we finally had electricity. It was surprising to find out we could live without the things we thought of as necessities. We learned this again in 1998, when the huge ice storm consumed Maine. We were without electricity for nine days. We had a small end-heater in the kitchen, and were blessed with our wood burning furnace in the basement. I wrapped potatoes in foil and laid them on the ring around the furnace, turning them frequently so they would not burn.

My brother Buddy came every other day with his generator, and gave us power to heat water, to take a shower, and the freezer ran so we did not lose our food. Kerosene lamps offered evening light, and we soon learned to go to bed with the chickens.

After enduring this inconvenience for a prolonged period, friends invited us to dinner for a hot meal. As we drove out the driveway we noticed the street lights were on. I said, "I think we have power."

Bruce said, "Quiet, I am going for a hot meal."

Poverty Level

This was before credit cards, but I was trying to get an account with a store, so I could put things on lay away. The clerk is asking me a series of questions: What is your annual income?

I told her.

She said, "Oh, my gosh, you are below the poverty level."

I said, "Tell me about it."

"Do you own or rent?"

"Own."

"How much is your mortgage?"

"I don't have a mortgage."

"That's impossible."

I told her, "No it isn't. We save our money, and when we have enough money to buy a box of nails, we put up more boards."

I don't think she believed me, so I got up and walked out the door.

It was after this incident I realized how my parents had prepared me to cope with the struggles of living with a limited income. Now, I was glad I knew how to plant a garden and preserve vegetables for the winter.

One of my fondest memories was making applesauce together with Mom and my sisters after we were married. Mom went to the orchard and picked up bushels of drops from under the apple tree. Bless her heart, she had washed two bushes of apples the day before, and was up very early cutting and coring the apples. She had two bushel ready and waiting for us to proceed with the sweet, sticky process. Everyone worked together like a well-oiled team, and shared the eighty quarts of pink applesauce which we enjoyed during the cold, snowy winter. Now we share this family task with our children.

Thanks to the many chores we had to do as a child, we were well prepared to leave home, and make it on our own. We have, in turn, taught our children with equally good results.

Maybe Mom didn't have a teaching degree, but she was a teacher extraordinaire.

I enjoyed teaching kindergarten and first grade for many years, and was principal for a while. I loved working with the children.

I had a young student ask," How do you spell wanna?"

I explained, "It wasn't really a word, but slang for want to."

"Help me spell gunna I'm gunna get a big ball for Christmas."

I said, "That is going to."

"No! I want the word gunna," he said.

I repeated, "It is going to."

He said, "I ain't going anywhere."

Diane

Diane was my fifth child, and the oldest was eight-years-old. She did not have the rosy, pudgy cheeks of her sister; I cried many times concerned for her as she followed in the footsteps of her beautiful older sister. It wasn't long before this ugly duckling turned into a magnificent swan. You can dress her in a potato sack and she is beautiful.

Diane tells the story of a monumental crisis in her young life:

The circus came to Cornish; I was very sick with the measles, and was unable to go. That was very difficult. Everybody went to the circus, and I was left in a dark room crying my eyes out. When they came home they brought me a small, red, metal telephone. It made a little tinkling ringing sound when I turned the dial. I was tickled with my phone. We usually did not get many toys. I never had anything like it. They also brought me a little, white, fluffy kitty that played music when I wound it up. It had the softest fur, and I was so proud of my kitty.

Terry decided to operate on the kitten to see what made the music. She went to the office, and found one of Dad's old scalpels to cut the cat open. I wanted to kill her. I was crushed. That was my kitty. Then she tried to stuff the music box back inside the cat, and suture it closed. But it was never the same.

Do you remember Buddy's story about the catfish? Well, that was another of my cat's nine lives.

One Sunday in late August the family arrived in Upton to find about three inches of snow on the ground. The high elevation was the contributing factor. Mom was unpacking the picnic basket when she realized Dad had not taken his medicine. She saw him at the end of the field. She gave me the medicine, and I went running barefoot through the field oblivious of the snow, until I was almost there. I stopped, and stood on a smooth, warm rock with one foot on the rock, and the other on top my foot. I looked like a flamingo. Daddy came to me, and took his medicine. He picked me up, put me on his shoulders, tucked my cold, bare feet into the pockets of his jacket, and carried me back to the house.

John, Buddy, and Scotte played in the elementary band in Fryeburg, but I wasn't old enough. They had baton lessons downstairs, so I took lessons while the band was practicing.

I was a majorette in the elementary school band. When I was older, I started playing the flute and took lessons from Mr. Fuchs. When I was in high school I had to fight to be a majorette. I went to the band director and I said, "What do I need to do to try out to be a majorette?"

He told me, "You don't have the right equipment."

I said, "What do you mean? I can twirl circles around these girls."

He kind of laughed about it then said, "You need a ten minute routine."

So I said, "Fine." I went home, and I worked, and worked on a routine all by myself. A couple weeks later I went to him and said, "I'm ready." He laughed at me again. I put on the music, and proceeded to do my routine. He was shocked, and surprised at my ability. So at this point he really had to let me be a majorette, because he knew I wasn't going away. The deal was when the band marched, I was a majorette, and when the band played in concert, I played the flute. That wasn't a problem. That was what I wanted anyways. Many of the girls did not have the opportunity to work with a good instructor. I was fortunate to have a good instructor while my brothers and sister were at band practice. I was playing the flute and organ by the time I was ten years old.

I still have my baton, and I pull it out every once in a while and twirl away, or toot my flute.

I asked, "What can't you tolerate?"

"I have no patience for kids horsing around in cars."

Is there anything out of the ordinary that you remember about your clothes?

I was always out of the ordinary. I made a lot of my clothes. We wore mostly dresses or skirts to school. Eventually, in high school I wore slacks occasionally.

Were you ever bullied or were you the bully?

"I was probably the bully." I teased Kim a lot when she was curious about why a dog lifted his leg to pee.

What was the worst thing you ever did?

Probably the time we ran out of balloons for our water-balloon fight. I went into Dad's stash of rubbers, and filled them with water. I asked, "Do you mean the little finger cots?"

Diane screamed with gales of laughter, "Oh, no, no, we're talking torpedoes." I was the envy of the neighborhood when I came out with those things filled with water.

What was the greatest gift you ever received?

"Life, country life."

What would you do if you won a million dollars?

After a long pause, "Anything I wanted to."

Would it change you?

"Probably not."

Who would you like to spend an afternoon with?

"John"

How did our working in the office affect you?

It was hard, because patients came first. But it was kind of neat, because we were able to see things like people with a chain saw cuts, and picking out the sawdust, or watching people's plantar warts being cut off, watching Dad put on a cast, and helping kids cut off their casts. There were a lot of interesting things.

It was kind of hard having the practice in the house. The way the house was laid out we had to walk right past the open stairwell to the waiting room to get in the bathroom, and people might be sitting on the stairs. It was embarrassing when I had to wrap myself in a towel, and run to my room. When Mother was busy she asked one of the patients to put our hair in curlers.

I remember the time Terry and I had been up to the Douglas' farm. When we came down the hill Terry crashed her bicycle; she went off the road into barbed wire, and was all torn up. Her bike was so twisted she was unable to ride it. I dabbed her bloody scratches, made her comfortable, and then I rode my bike home for help.

The waiting room was packed, and I knew patients came first, so I left my bike at home, and ran over half a mile back to my sister. I helped her to her feet, and then struggle to get the crippled bicycle out of the ditch. I don't know which wobbled more, my sister or the crumpled bike. I finally made it home supporting my wounded sister, and wheeling the disabled square-wheeled bike.

Even though our parents were at home, it was times like this that we felt all alone—remembering that the patients came first. It was hard.

Diane's first money making project was picking blueberries interspersed with playing. She picked blueberries all weekend then cleaned and sorted them, and sold them as soon as we came home for the whopping sum of one dollar a quart.

When she was about eight years old she inherited her next job from her older sister. She received the privilege of pulling weeds from Lydia's flower bed. She soon learned why her sister had been so generous, and she came to dislike the job also.

Lydia lived in a well-kept white one-story house surrounded by colorful, sweet-smelling flower beds. Her arthritic back did not allow her to do the excessive bending to pull the weeds. The young girls were closer to the ground, and were always pleased to earn a few cents. It was more fun to work for someone else, and earn a quarter or two, than to stay home, and work for Mother for no pay.

Lydia kept a close eye on Diane, and brought her a cold drink of cranberry juice at snack time. Diane shivered as she drank the tangy, crimson drink. Lydia smiled, and reassured her that cranberry juice was good for her kidneys. Diane didn't know what her kidneys were, but she preferred a cold soda-pop.

Family

I asked Diane what she remembered about her grandparents.

I was only four years old when Grandpa Barnes died, but I remember he liked to tease me. He would reach for my long blond hair and say, "Come here and let me cut off some of your shiny hair, so I can use it to make new shiny fish lures." I was scared he would cut off my pony tail. He didn't want anyone else to sit in his chair, and he used the word Jesus a lot. That is about all I can remember.

I have many memories of Grandma Rose Barnes. I can still smell the hot applesauce cooking on her stove, and the apple pies in the oven. She was always humming as she went about her work. I asked her why she hummed and she told me, "When Grandpa had his heart attack over fifteen years ago; he was afraid of being alone, and wanted to know where I was. I couldn't sit with him all the time as I had housework to do and cooking, so I started humming. It made him feel secure knowing I was nearby."

I remember one time we were at her place swimming, and when we came to her house she made us take off our wet bathing suits. It wasn't long before we wanted to go swimming again. She wouldn't let us put on our cold, wet suits, so she put them in the oven to dry them out. I can still smell those raunchy suits baking in the oven.

One day we were visiting, and she wanted to make drop eggs on toast. She got the eggs going, but forgot she didn't have any bread. She would not let us walk to the store by ourselves. She turned the eggs down to low on the stove, and all of us went to the store, two houses away, to get bread. When we got back, the eggs had exploded; they were on the cupboards, ceiling, and everywhere.

I remember the day she wanted to kill me. We were swimming at Sebago, and Scotte dove off a big rock and hit bottom. It knocked her braces loose, and when she came up all I could see was blood and the braces. I thought she had broken off all her teeth. I ran to the house crying, and Grandma got in the car, and drove down to the beach; she found things were not as bad as I portrayed.

She was always the teacher. One day she took Scotte, Terry, and me out in the woods in Upton. She got us all twisted around. She leaned up against a rock, and said she didn't know where the house was. How were we going to find it? Where was the sun when we walked in, etc. It was a lifesaving lesson we never forgot.

After Grandpa died, she learned how to drive a car. She was so short she had to sit on a pillow, and still she could not see over the steering wheel; she had to peek through the steering wheel to see to drive.

We saw Grandpa and Grandma Barnes every week, but got to see Grandpa and Grandma Freese only a couple times a year. We never knew when they were coming; we would open the door, and there they were. Grandpa climbed the mountain with us, and he took us for rides on his motorcycle.

He was so proud of his garden in Ohio. One day he picked a huge pan of strawberries, and Grandma made biscuits for shortcake. He kept telling us we needed to use more strawberries. He didn't want to see any biscuit. A memory we never forgot.

He tried to show us things we had never seen before, and one Sunday he took us to the Goodyear Aerospace Hanger. It was a huge building, so big you could fly an airplane in one end and out the other. He tried to get us to walk to the other end, but we didn't have time before dark.

Grandma Freese was very quiet, very petite, and enjoyed her needlework. She cooked really good meals, and had a cute little giggle. I could not understand why she was sleeping downstairs. I didn't know how sick she was, and that she didn't have the strength to climb the stairs. There was so much love between her and Grandpa. She made me smile.

Tall slender Diane didn't have much of a chance with her older siblings, but her charm won them over.

Childhood Memories

Diane relates some stories of her early childhood:

When you were busy in the office we used to sit on our bed pillows and slide down the attic steps. I liked to use Billy's pillow. I didn't want to use my pillow! Yughhhh! His room was on the third floor, and once I made it to the top of the steps, it only made sense to use his pillow for the ride down the steps.

Billy taught me to ride a dirt bike when I was about twelve. I was wearing my favorite "cool", bell-bottom jeans. Buddy was riding a bigger bike, and he didn't know I could ride at all. He started yelling at me; I stalled the bike, and I had trouble starting it. Finally, it started and I took off, but my ankle was smashed against the bike. The bottom of my jeans got caught in the chain. Buddy wanted to take a knife and cut them off. I was crying, because they were my favorite pair of jeans. There wasn't much we could do. We tried lifting the back of the motorcycle up, and spinning the wheel backwards and tugging and twisting, but we could not get the pants loose from the chain, so he finally had to cut off my jeans.

Tell me some stories about John

John had an eight-track player. He loaded the car full of us kids, and half of the neighbors to take us swimming. I don't know how he had patience with all the music, yelling, and so forth, but that was John. Buddy was always looking for the short-cut, but John used his brain to think things through. He had to make a plan, whether we were building a snow fort or chopping down a tree. John always had the adult view. He was always looking after us girls. One day we had a flat tire on the car; he made us go stand in the ditch away from the car while he changed the tire. There are many memories like scuba diving, and places he took us. Buddy was more the animal toward us girls, probably because we were closer in age.

We were on vacation in Newfoundland staying in the log cabin we had built a few years before. We were going to go to the Honky-Tonk with Dean's kids, Darcy, Wilson, and Macy. John, Buddy, Neil, Scotte, Terry, and I were going to show them how to play pool. It was quite a hike from the cabin, almost four miles. The boys were ahead of us. Buddy got to the road first, and he hid in the ditch; every time a car passed, he would jump out of the ditch. While he was hiding John and Neil passed him. We girls decided to stick together. Eventually, we passed Buddy hiding in the ditch. After a while Buddy jumped out at a truck. The fellow stopped, and asked if he wanted a ride, so Buddy hopped in. When they got close to us Buddy asked, "Would you mind picking them up? They are my sisters." We hopped in the back of the truck. Pretty soon they came to Neil; Buddy asked him to stop for his brother, and Neil got in back with us.

The speck way ahead was John. When the truck got closer to him, Buddy didn't say anything. All of us started yelling, "That's our brother, stop."

Buddy said, "No, can't be," but the man stopped anyways, and picked up John. Buddy was bragging about where we would be if he had not saved the day.

He decided if a two-seater stopped on our way back, he was going to get in the seat, and the rest of us would have to walk.

I asked, "How did John's death affect you?"

It was very hard. We couldn't do anything. He was such an important part of the family. He was the glue that held us together. There was too much hurt. I didn't want anyone, just stay away from me. He was a hard shadow for me to follow. I always thought Dad wanted me to take on John's role. That was a lot of pressure. He said, "You are just like him. He was going to be a doctor, so you should be a doctor." I was accepted at Orono in pre-med and I went to orientation. I went out partying, and when I got back to the dorm, I couldn't get in. I didn't know there was a curfew. I started knocking on windows, and finally someone let me it. My heart was not in being a doctor, but I would give up my life to do what made somebody else happy.

I stopped at Westbrook College on the way home, because I was interested in design. I really wanted to go to school at the Rhode Island School of Design. One of my teachers set up an interview with someone that had a shop in the Old Port section. She would have liked me join her, but unfortunately it was commission work only. I was just out of college. I had an apartment and responsibilities, and I didn't know if I would even be able to eat. I don't know where I could have gone designing.

Stories of Scotte

Scotte was our taxi. She had the old jeep station wagon; that was her jeep. She was very careful driving it, and she was specific as to what she expected of her passengers.

Scotte took me to Ft. Fairfield when I was the Apple Queen. This was a big event. Scotte and I were on our own. We drove and drove. It is a long ways, but we finally got there. We thought Hiram was small, but this town was smaller. It was one road, and it lasted maybe six buildings, including a restaurant and hotel. We had quite a chuckle about that.

They had a hospitality room where all the princesses met each other, and received instructions for the parade the next morning. We didn't know where we were going to spend the night.

One of the girls said she had a pool at her house, and she invited everyone to stay there. This girl was weird as a three-dollar bill. Sotte and I looked at each other, and we decided we didn't want to spend any more time with her.

I went to the bathroom, and took a long time. The plan was to be the last one to leave the room, and then we would have the key to the hospitality room. We managed to linger long enough that we had the key, and therefore possession of the room.

We went to the gas station to gas up the car. I was rather timid, but Scotte being two years older started talking with a couple airmen. We had never seen an air force base. Before I knew it we were in their car headed for the air force base. I was nervous, but we went on and saw Loring Air Force Base. And then they turned around and brought us back.

By now it was time for bed. We snuck into the hotel, up the stairs, took showers, and tried to sleep. We knew what time they would be back at the hospitality room in the morning, but we could not leave a wakeup call because we were not supposed to be in the room. We didn't have an alarm clock, so I didn't know if I could sleep. It was about twelve-thirty when we got to our room. I woke up about five o'clock, and I woke Scotte, "Hurry, get up, we have to get dressed, and be sitting in the chairs when they get here." We washed up, and I put on my formal gown, sash and crown. We folded the towels, made the bed to perfection, and were sitting nonchalantly in the chairs when the others arrived. We didn't have anything to eat, but when they started arriving we carried it off, and no one knew we slept there that night.

After the parade was over we headed for home. We decided to never tell anyone about our spending the night in the hotel.

Stories of Terry

Terry and I had to share a room for a long time. I kept my part clean, but she was a pig. She would trash the room, and then world war three would break out. Scotte would come to rescue her. She would sit on me to get things under control, and then she would let Terry tickle my feet.

One day I was really mad at both of them and I decided to run away from home.

Neil fit right into the family. He could think of things we had never tried. He always had us laughing. He was the first person I ever saw swim across the river at Jump City, and then swim back. I remember the time in Upton when he showed us how to hold the broom upside down in front of our face, and to keep spinning around. Soon all of us were lying on the ground in convulsions.

My kids never had a chance to do some of the things I experienced when I was growing up. We all got in the boat, and John took us to Jump City. When Neil was here in 1971 it was popular for everything to be named with city tacked on the end. Jump City was a steep sandy bank on the Saco River. You would go back about 15 feet from the edge, run forward, and jump. You were to land upright on your feet, and then you were to run down this cliff. If you fell, you had sand in places you did not want. We would spend hours a day playing there. When we were little, we only went part way up and then jumped. Eventually, we worked up our courage to go to the top. It was great when we had the boat there, we could go home wet, but not sandy. If we drove in the car, we would be wet, and covered with sand.

Words

Dad was a proponent of enlarging the kid's vocabulary. He wrote new words all over the house expecting the children to use them in a sentence after they researched the meaning. Diane reached for the baby powder after her shower, and in big letters she saw T E D I O U S. She didn't know what the word meant, and was scared to use the powder for fear it might a flea powder dad had put in the powder can to use on the dogs. She did not use the powder until she looked the word up in the dictionary. She never forgot that word. A week later she reached for the box of sanitary napkins and saw more big black letters I N S I D I O U S. She didn't care if she died of a poison, she needed that napkin NOW.

Tell me about cheerleading.

I yelled loud enough, so we didn't need many more girls in the team. I had learned to do cartwheels in my dancing lessons, and by the time I was in high school. I was the only girl that did cartwheels the entire length of the basketball court. When we tried pyramids, I was the top person.

There was a foul shooting contest, and all of the basketball girls participated, of course I was a cheerleader at that time. I shot for the hoop whenever I was waiting, whether for the cheerleading coach or other girls on the cheerleading squad. One year I entered the competition, and made 48 out of 50 foul shots. The basketball coaches wanted me to leave the cheerleading squad and join the basketball team.

One of my duties as captain of the cheerleader squad was to announce the names of the players of both teams. I used a normal voice for the visiting team and then a booming voice for our hometown heroes.

There was a five day cheerleading camp at Colby College. All of the girls wanted to go, but it was costly, and many parents could not afford to send their girls. My feeling was, it is all or none, so we spent the whole year fund raising. We had bake sales, car washes, and things like that. I crocheted an afghan that we raffled off. We did a lot of candied apples, caramel apples, and popcorn sales after school. There were ten of us girls that went, and not a parent had put a nickel out. It was quite an experience.

First Jobs

The twenty acres of low-bush blueberries were full of plump blue orbs waiting to be picked. The children were expected to pick blueberries on Sundays, so they had enough to sell to their regular customers on Monday. When I was not busy cooking or doing dishes I picked berries to make pies, and to have berries for a blueberry cake which I baked every day.

One week when the berry picking was at its best, and the girls were older, they stayed alone all week to pick berries, and to charge people who came to pick during the week. The store owner drove up on the mountain to check on the girls if they had not made a trip to the store.

There was a horrendous thunder storm that week. The girls remembered hearing the story of the previous house being struck by lightning, and burning to the ground. They were extremely scared, and didn't want to be hit by lightning. The three of them went upstairs, and hid under Grandma's bed. They protected Terry, the youngest one, by putting her against the wall. Diane and Scotte huddled around her to shield her from the lightning and thunder. It was so loud that they covered their ears. When the noisy thunder ceased, they slowly crawled out from their sheltered nest, and crept downstairs quietly. They didn't want to wake the thunderous creature. After the rain stopped they went outside, and saw the copper rod, which was the ground for the lightning rods, had been lifted a foot and one-half out of the ground. When their dad arrived

Saturday he explained lightning had struck the house, and the copper rod saved their lives.

I took the older kids to the ski slopes every Tuesday for class lessons. Diane was six years old, and she started preparing supper as soon as she came home from school. The menu was always the same—spaghetti and Jello with fruit. Diane had to carry her stool from sink to stove to table. She got more exercise climbing up, and down on her stool than the skiers did on the slopes.

She added frozen blueberries and frozen wild raspberries to the Jello so it was set firm by supper time. She opened the refrigerator door, and blocked it with a chair until she put the Jello on the shelf. She muttered to herself, "I will be glad when I am big enough to reach things, and won't have to carry the stool around."

That took care of dessert for supper, now it was time to make the spaghetti sauce. There were no jars of sauce at that time, but she opened an envelope of dehydrated ingredients, added water, and simmered this until it thickened into a perfect sauce. The big pan filled with water was on the stove, and as I drove in the driveway, she turned on the burner. As soon as the water was boiling I added the spaghetti. Everyone helped set the table, and within ten minutes we were eating. Diane did this every week.

The girls were baking at a young age. Little Diane found the recipe for toll house cookies and proceeded to make them all by herself. She served them for supper, and they did not resemble my cookies. I had her bring the recipe to me and tell me what she did.

"I measured one cup sugar, one-half cup brown sugar, one and one-half sticks of oleo, and I beat this together, and then added the eggs. The recipe said cream, but it didn't tell me how much and we didn't have any cream, so I added one-half cup milk, and then added the flour, salt, baking soda, and vanilla. The cookies were soft and delicious, so we wrote down Diane's recipe and titled it "Diane's Cookies."

The three girls took tap and ballet lessons. I had to take Buddy with us and the teacher had him participate in the warm-up stretches and summer-saults. They gave a recital at the end of the year; each girl did two or three dances. Costumes were expensive, and soon I was the wardrobe mother. I made all of the costumes for all the students.

Diane was knitting by the time she was in the second grade. Each grade participated in the Christmas program. Diane sat in her chair knitting while others performed.

When Diane's class was up front singing, I entered into a fracas with a neighbor. She spotted the knitting setting on Diane's chair and confiscated it. I told her to put it back, because it was a prop for their play. Diane was the Grandma sitting in her rocker knitting as the story was performed.

By the time Diane was ten years old she had completed knitting white cable knee-socks of light weight sport yarn, and a sweater.

Entrepreneur

At the age of ten Diane became an entrepreneur. She had watched me make breakfast rolls, and she knew they were a big seller at the church bake sale. She proposed the idea of her making, and selling breakfast rolls. I encouraged her; however, as the owner of a business I explained she had to purchase the materials to make the rolls. After lengthy negotiations it was decided Diane was responsible for purchasing the flour and yeast, and I donated the other ingredients, the use of the kitchen, and oven. Diane had to sign a promissory note for the cost of a twenty-five pound bag of flour and twelve packets of dry yeast needed to start her business. She was to repay the loan from her first sales, and by then she had accumulated enough capital to purchase her next supplies. I explained the contract in detail, so Diane understood there would be no profits from the first few baking's of her prized confection.

Diane was so excited she hardly slept. She wanted to get up very early to make the dough for the rolls. Five o'clock in the morning arrived, and her feelings had changed; she wanted to sleep, but she dressed and went to the kitchen while the entire household slept.

When the dough was ready to knead she retrieved her stool, so she stood above her work kneading it back and forth, stroke after stroke, finally the dough had that different feel and it was ready to be put in the greased pan to rise.

Now the waiting began; she was alone and the house was still quiet. She would wash her dishes later; right now she was going to take a nap on the couch.

When the family came downstairs she shuffled to the kitchen to sneak a peek under the towel covering the dough; it hadn't raised much. I suggested she fill pans with hot water, and place them touching the four side of the pan of dough. She stole another peek after breakfast and was happy to see the dough starting to rise. After eating breakfast, washing the dishes, and making the beds I told Diane it was time to punch the dough down, turn it over, cover it, and wait for the yeast to work. Diane's anticipation turned to discouragement because it was taking so long. I suggested, "This is a good time for you to get your baking sheets ready, lay out the butter, brown sugar and nutmeg to be ready for the next step." Soon it was time to roll out half of the dough, spread it with butter, sprinkle brown sugar evenly on the dough, and finally sprinkle on the nutmeg. It was cumbersome trying to roll the log, but finally it lay across the middle of the pastry board in a neat row. I taught her how to mark the log in half, and then quarters before she started cutting. This helped her keep the slices a uniform size. As she cut, she laid the slices on the cookie sheets giving them room to grow.

She stood back, and with a feeling of pride she covered the final baking sheet with a clean towel. More waiting, but she stayed busy; first she cleaned up the pastry board and tools, then she gathered the ingredients to make the frosting. When the frosting was completed she peeked, and was delighted to see the rolls were ready to bake. She slid the pans into the preheated oven, and set the timer. They will be ready soon; she brought the picnic basket from the basement, and wiped the inside to make sure there were no spider webs.

Suddenly, she remembered she might need some change, and the hunt was on, looking for dimes and quarters. She ran to the kitchen when she heard the timer ring; she opened the oven and the rolls were pale, they needed a couple more minutes to brown. She had the holders in hand when she heard the timer ding again, and a smile came across her face as she opened the oven door and saw perfection. The baked rolls were removed, and the next pans were put in to bake. She carefully separated six rolls, and moved them to a rack to cool. The brown sugar had melted and caused the rolls to stick to the pan, but that was the delicious part.

Now, she had to speed up; she quickly washed and dried the cookie sheets. She frosted the groups of six buns, one group at a time, and moved them to the clean pans. She removed the hot pastries from the oven, and then they were frosted. She was tired, but no time to slow down. She started wrapping the first group with wax paper, and placing them in the picnic basket. When the second group had been prepared she grabbed her change, and the picnic basket and headed for the camp grounds a short distance away. Fear was setting in; she had not considered sales in her business plan.

A nine year old boy rushed out to greet her. "What is in the basket?" he asked. She opened the basket and when he saw the delicious morsels he quickly said, "Don't go to that trailer; she's on a diet. Go to the next one; that's where I live." After the sale he ran ahead of Diane heralding her wares, and soon the basket was empty, but after each sale she promised to return. When she returned home she counted her money, looked at the promissory note, and decided she was in business.

One day near the end of her deliveries, she tripped and fell. A half dozen rolls tumbled out of the basket into the dirt and sand; she stood up, wiped off her knees, picked up the rolls, and ran home with tears streaming down her face. She was devastated at the setback, and wanted to quit, but her financial backer refused to allow that. She pursued this job for a couple years in between her other adventures.

The neighborhood girls were envious of her, and wanted the recipe. As Diane was writing down the recipe she asked. "Is it okay to leave out the yeast?" I said no, because they will not be able to make them. They tried, but their rolls resembled hockey pucks.

She made rolls to enter the exhibits at the Oxford County Fair. The book said the prize was $5.00 for the winner in the adult division and $3.00 for entrants under twelve. I spoke with the secretary to make out the registration form. When she found out Diane was ten, she said she will have to be in the junior division. I said, "No there is nothing saying she cannot enter the adult division and that was the category we want and, she is going to take first place." She was entered, judged, and she did win first place receiving a blue ribbon and $5.00.

April vacation was rapidly approaching and the Barnes girls did not have employment lined up, so I stepped up to find a job for them. This was not to keep them out of my hair, but I considered it a pre-graduate course in financial education. They learned the elusive answer as to what it takes to earn the all mighty buck.

I telephoned the owner of Fryeburg Nursery, a company that grew evergreen seedlings, and told him I had three daughters and two neighborhood boys seeking employment during the April vacation. He said, "I don't have openings for that many in the plant."

I quickly responded, "I want them working in the field, so they will learn where the almighty dollar comes from." I was told to have them in Fryeburg at seven o'clock Saturday morning with a bag lunch.

The following is Diane's slant on this job:

Every morning it was the same thing. A man climbed onto the back up the truck and asked, "Are there any college graduates? Is there anybody that ever went to college? Are any of you high school graduates?" There was a conglomerate of people. "Is there anybody in high school?" I saw a hand go up for the first time, and it was my sister's. I felt like I was starring in *Roots*. After the roll call and inquisition we were loaded onto trailers military style, and off we went.

There were drunks, an old man with only three teeth, and other derelicts. They drove all of us out to the field; put the drunks and derelicts in one field, and took us away to another. As we climbed off of the trailers the announcer yelled repeatedly, "Pull up the trees, tie twenty-five in a bundle, and bury the roots!" Other men would pick them up later. "Pull up the trees, twenty-five in a bundle, and bury the roots!" I heard that chant in my dreams that night.

I thought my life was coming to an end. Finally, it was lunch time. I looked at my hands and there was no way I could eat my lunch with those filthy hands. I HAD TO WASH THEM. My lunch break was spent searching for the Saco River to wash my hands, and returning just in time to hear them say, "Back to the field. Pull up the trees, twenty-five in a bundle, and bury the roots."

The next day Scotte was told she was to go inside, and not to get on the truck. I was panicky. My sister was being taken somewhere else. Where were they taking her? I was put on the truck and taken to the field. She worked inside. I went to the field. It didn't take me as long that day to find the river to wash my hands. While in the field, I was thinking about Scotte. I flashed back to hearing *The Jefferson's* theme song, "Movin' on up to the east side to the apartment in the sky." I figured that was where Scotte went, and I wanted to go there too.

I was moved inside on the third day. I thought that my prayers had been answered; I was delighted. I was on the assembly line. I was told to cut the twine, and open the bundles. I didn't know where they went, and I didn't care.

It was really cold inside, and I was dressed to be in the field with the sun beating on me. I was shivering, and shaking by the end of the day from the cold. The next day I dressed for it. That was an interesting experience. I really learned the importance of an education. Without it you would be doing work like this for the rest of your life. Probably, the funniest thing was Sam and Steve continued working there after our week was up. I looked at them and asked, "Are you kids not normal?"

It was the worst; I had enough of that. It felt so good to be back in school, studying.

Diane's first summer employment was working at Stone Ridge Restaurant washing dishes. In the morning she had to vacuum the lounge downstairs, and clean the apartment upstairs, and then it was lunch time. She scraped the plates, and put them in the dish washer. Then, she was promoted to being the salad girl.

She was the new kid on the block so she had the privilege of washing the floor. It was always her turn to wash the floor. It was her turn to wash the pots and pans. It was always her turn to wash the pots and pans. It was another step in her education. She was peeling potatoes, and getting things ready for supper. She was busy, busy, not a moment to waste.

Diane tells:

One night a couple lingered late into the evening. The restaurant closed at ten o'clock, but they stayed and stayed. I washed all of the pots and pans, but I wasn't allowed to wash the floor until after they left. They stayed until eleven-thirty. When they left, and I was cleaning up their mess I found they had left me twenty-five dollars. That was a pretty good tip for a dishwasher.

It was a good job. I spent the entire day there, and sometimes when I had all my work finished I lay on a blanket in the sun out near the woods. Scotte played the organ and I did a variety of jobs. Before I left I checked with the bar down stairs to see if they needed more ice. There was one time when Scotte and I snuck downstairs to hear the band playing. Pretty soon Scotte and I are out on the dance floor having a great time, acting crazy. We were hauled upstairs, and Brad, the manager, wanted to smell our breath. "You girls can't dance, and act that silly if you aren't inebriated".

We weren't; that was just us. My defense was, "You know my mother don't you? I rest my case."

One day I cut my finger badly, and I passed out; when I came to I was on the floor, and everyone was around me. I asked what happened as I sat up. They told me I cut my finger, and I looked at my finger, and passed out again. Next time they covered the finger.

The next year I was a waitress. Some nights I also had to tend bar, but needed to ask one of the older waitresses to serve the drinks.

Buddy was hired as an assistant chef, and the owner's wife did not know about it. Buddy did not know who she was, and one evening she stopped in to make her little surprise visit. The two of them pranced around the kitchen, each trying to dislodge the other as unwanted intruders.

Soon, Buddy was working as the chef. On the Fourth of July we bought a big watermelon and put it in the cooler, and infused it with vodka. The owner's wife stopped in for a surprise inspection. She asked why the watermelon was in the cooler. I thought quickly and said, "We thought a small piece on the plate would make a nice decoration."

"Oh, good idea," she responded. Buddy was breaking up. Somebody went out back, and knocked over a can of green beans. She was so nosey she had to check it out—completely diverting her from the watermelon.

I was hired at another restaurant in Cornish to wait on tables. I bought a new white uniform, and reported to work. They put me to work peeling potatoes. I did not have a problem peeling potatoes, but there was no apron, and it ruined her new uniform. I was hired as a waitress, and expected them to live up to their word. I did not want to work for someone that was so fickle, so I quit at the end of that day.

College

I was surprised by the college students. They were so upper class, and I didn't click with many of them. It was a girl's school, and on a nice warm day lots of girls went go out in their bikinis to lay in the yard. There were some weirdoes that thought it was free viewing, and a couple girls had complained. I said, "Time to take the bull by the horns" I went to the drug store and bought a package of balloons. They were all looking at me strangely, and into the bathroom I went. "I need a clothes basket, get me a clothes basket." The girls dumped their clothes out, and brought me their clothes baskets. I started putting the balloons on the spigot, and they said, "Oh wow, that's one way to get rid of him." We loaded five clothes baskets, and opened the window by the fire escape where this guy is standing. We also had three other windows opened, and we positioned ourselves. Boy did we plaster that guy. He didn't stand a chance.

When I was in college I worked at Ski Togs on Sundays, and I was also the Tupperware Lady. I was juggling the three jobs. Plus full time school. The first year I was on campus I had to be a proctor; I called it babysitting the dorms that allowed male visitors.

I was in a dorm that didn't, but I was in some trouble because I did speak my mind. They didn't pay me to proctor, so I went to the Dean's office and I said, "If I am on a schedule to work, I am going to work, and I will not be available to baby sit in someone else's dorm, because I am paying you for my education, therefore if you want to pay me for the babysitting job, fine, if not I am not going to do it." There was quite a bit of hubbub because I refused to do it.

The other girls received seventy-five to two hundred dollars a week for spending money, and that wasn't the way I was taught. We worked for what we had. So, I left staying on campus. I preferred to work three jobs, and pay rent rather than live on campus. The first apartment had three of us on the third floor, then we moved down to a larger apartment on the second floor; there were five of us living on Congress Street. Two of the people working nights so it was like rotating beds. It was a little disgusting when you think about it. Especially, one of the guys didn't have the best of hygiene. But it was what it was.

It was near a Seven-Eleven. One night I walked down the street to get milk from the store, and the next thing I knew a cop stopped me, and blocked my way. He was asking me all kind of questions. I didn't understand why they were talking with me, so I answered his questions. I bought the milk, and when I returned to the apartment, I was telling these "city-wise" girls about it, and they said, "Oh my God, Diane don't you know what they were doing?"

"No"

"They thought you were a prostitute."

"A what?" It never even occurred to me. I had been told, 'It takes a country person two weeks to learn city, but it takes a city person at least two years, and a night light burning, to learn what it means to be country.' The light came on, and burned brightly for the rest of my stay in Portland. That arrangement lasted about six months.

Then I rented an apartment on Washington Avenue. It was in the upstairs of a little house. Johnny and his wife lived downstairs. It was the neatest thing. He had hot chocolate ready for me when I came home from working. His wife passed away while I was living there which was hard. Johnny and I became really good friends. He went roller skating twice a week. He never had a driver's license, so I often took him grocery shopping.

Diane had a job at Sears & Roebuck while she went to college. She started in the towel, sheet, and linen department; that was boring. She then moved to the Ladies Fashion Department; she didn't click with the other employees. Diane was about serving the customers, and the other girls were competing with each other about the clothes they were wearing and who could out do the other. She then transferred to the Men's Department, and she loved that. There was a lot of busy work, always a lot of stocking to do, and keeping the area neat. When a man wanted a shirt she didn't have to measure him, she knew the size he wore. She worked there quite a while.

A man bought two pair of pants and the tailor marked them to be shortened, and he told the customer they would be ready in two weeks, but he needed them sooner. Diane whispered to him, "I can do them tonight. Pay for them—leave the store—come back and when they aren't looking, lay down the bag. I will hand you note with my name, address, and phone number. You can come back in tomorrow night, and I will have them ready for you." When he came in to pick up his trousers he asked how much he owed her.

Diane said, "Two dollars each," meaning each pair, and the man handed her eight dollars, meaning two dollars per leg. She had to be careful about things like that.

We were taught to SAVE, SAVE, SAVE, spend wisely. I fought with Sears to get a Sears credit card, just because I wanted to establish credit, and they kept denying me. Several times I said, "I am an employee of yours and you're denying me, maybe I need more hours." Finally, I received my Sears card.

Then I received an offer, in the mail, for an American Express card, so I thought 'Oh my, this is easy.' I filled it out and received my American Express card. This is great, when I need something, I charge it, but nobody told me how to use a credit card wisely. When I realized how the interest grew I paid it off, and cancelled my American Express Card. The credit card companies hate me because the full amount is paid the minute I receive the bill. They make no interest on me, and yet I get rewards for using the card.

I worked part time at Sears and part time at a women's clothing shop, and worked on Sundays at another store.

The woman's clothing store offered me a full-time assistant manager position in Boston. I checked it out, but expenses were so high I refused the job. They told me I no longer had a job with their company. Sears felt I was working for a competitor. I told them I didn't see how selling men's ware competed with women's clothing. Both jobs were gone.

Within two weeks I was working for Ventrex. I loved that, and advanced to operations supervisor.

Ventrex

The president of Ventrex Laboratories was signing us up to use their services, and I mentioned I had a daughter that had just graduated from college, and asked if he had a job for her, or if he knew of an opening. He gave me his card, and said she should call him for an appointment for an interview.

The next week at the State Medical Convention he stopped to visit with us. He noticed our photo album; he picked it up, and looked at the pictures. He came to a picture of six-year-old Diane dressed in her bunny dance costume with floppy ears and a puffy tail.

He asked, "May I borrow this picture for a while? I'll get it back to you in a few days."

The next week Diane went for her interview dressed very professionally. She felt the interview went well. As she stood to leave, Mr. McCavoy said, "There is just one thing. We have a rather strict dress code here, and I cannot allow anything like this," as he slapped the photo of the bunny costume onto the desk.

Diane stood and exclaimed, "I'll kill my mother, kill her dead!" Art laughed and said, "Can you report for work at eight o'clock Monday?"

I loved the job at Ventrex. There was a lot to learn about blood; marketing services, and managing employees.

There was one time when Portland had a terrible, terrible snow storm, and at that time I was working for Ventrex, a medical lab, and Johnny opened the door and said, "You are not going anywhere. You can't drive in this mess."

I said, "No problem, Johnny, I am going to ski to work." He said, "That's okay, you can ski to work, but you can't drive." It was about a mile, and I took off on my downhill skis, not cross county, and arrived at work only to find a drift in front of the door about five feet high. I had no shovel, so I dug my way in using my hands to get to the front door. The phone rang about thirty minutes later. It was Art the president of Ventrex. He said, "I knew if there was any darn fool that would be there, it would be you."

"Yes, that is me." He said he couldn't make it in, but I could telephone him at home if I needed him. That was a good job.

I was there for five years. I left, because I could not play favorites. We had a meeting, and I was told if a currier calls in sick they were to bring the company vehicle in so a substitute driver could use it. However, if Myrtle called in sick, she could keep the car.

The curriers were my responsibility. To me a policy is a policy the same for everyone. I excused myself from the meeting, and went out into the hallway. I was so angry that I made a fist, and I put it through the sheetrock. I gave my notice, and three month later I am still there, because my employees had vacations, and if I left it would have made a lot more work for the others. I finally said, "No, I am leaving." Shortly after I left they lost another five employees, because I was the kind of manager that helped out if we were swamped with work, and I worked with them. If they had to work overtime, I sent one person to get pizza, and we made a party out of it. Everyone just worked, worked, worked. The new manager came in, sat in her office, and barked orders. She would not lower herself by working next to her subjects. They had a big turnover.

Follow my Lead

I met Ellen while I was working at Ventrex, what a corker! We had so much fun. She knew where the best food was, and the time of their Happy Hour.

We could go out, get a drink for a dollar, and eat like a king for maybe two bucks. It was like a smorgasbord. There were all kinds of food from Swedish meatballs to fried rice. I said to her, "You mean I have been missing this all my life."

One night Ellen said, "Let's go down to the waterfront." The largest yacht I had ever seen was docked at the pier. She said, "Follow my lead."

When she said that, I should have run. She got me in so much trouble. There were men working on the magnificent yacht. She yelled up to them, "We were talking with the owners at Demillos restaurant. They said you would give us a tour of the ship if we came down, and spoke with you." She knew where the owners were, and they weren't coming back for a while.

"Come aboard," they beckoned. The fixtures for the hot and cold water were gold. I thought I had died, and gone to another planet. There were twenty-two bedrooms. This was somebody's private yacht. It was unbelievable. We left and giggled, "Tee-hee, tee-hee." How can you beat that?

Again I heard, "Follow my lead. Have you ever heard of the Underground?"

"Nope."

"You're going to love it." Ellen and I had a hard time going out to bars where there were bands, because we were two nice looking women, and we were constantly being pestered. Neither of us liked that. Soon we knew the bouncers pretty well, and all we had to do was just wink at them, and somebody would be escorted off. This night we went to the Underground. There was something different about this place; I couldn't figure it out. It was different, really different.

We sat at the bar, and ordered a drink. "What's the scoop?" I asked, "There are guys out on the dance floor with guys."

She said, "Yep, keep looking." I sat there watching everything.

The next thing I knew, two drinks showed up on the bar in front of us. I looked at Ellen and said, "Did you order these?"

"No. You didn't?"

"Nope," I said with a quizzical look on my face. She was playing with me like a cat with a mouse. She knew.

Ellen said, "Look around the place." I am looking around, studying the different characters. I looked down at the end of the bar, and there were two burly females sitting down there waiting, like vultures.

"Oh, what in hell have you got me into?" I now realized it was a gay bar.

She said, "Just go with it. Just go with it." A little while later I had to go to the restroom.

I wondered if it would be safer to go to the men's room. I started for the restroom, and the front door opened. Several people came in, and one of them was my sister, Teresa Rose. She said "What in tarnation are you doing here?"

I said, "I guess you have some explaining to do too." She came in with Warren and Steve, two gay fellows from our hometown.

She said, "I love this place." Anyways, it turned out to be a favorite haunt because we could go there, and guys wouldn't hassle us, but you had to watch out for the burly one.

I did get in trouble once. There was this nice looking guy; he was so sweet. He finished dancing, and came back to the bar. They started playing another song, and I said, "Would you like to dance?"

He looked at me and said, "No."

"Come on, let's go dance."

"No!"

Three or four minutes later the bouncer came over and said, "You! Out of here!"

"Me? Little old me, what did I do?"

"You're harassing the cliental."

Gas Company

I made sure I had another job before I left Ventrex. I took a job in Customer Service at Northern Utilities Gas Company. I didn't know anything about natural gas, but I enjoyed learning. I had never been a union employee. It didn't bother me at first, but one of the girls that had the same job as I did, thought it meant she could come to work at eight o'clock, sit at her desk, file her nails, and thirty minutes later turn on her computer. This was a bit of a challenge for me. She had a union card, so it didn't matter how little she worked.

Probably, the best day I had was when I went out on a trouble call with an older gentleman. Cliff was about two months from retirement. I wanted to see what these guys had to do when they had a trouble call. It was on the job training. The other two women did not want to do it, but I did. We received a call that one of the apartment complexes could smell gas. We found a construction worker had cut into a six-inch pipe, and there was gas everywhere.

Cliff climbed over the pile of dirt, and I am right on his heels. We found the shut-off valve to the six-inch pipe; it was almost like a faucet. Someone had painted it, and we couldn't get it closed. So, I grabbed ahold of it, and both of us tried to turn it, but we still couldn't budge it. He said, "Grab a rock!" Now that I think about it, that was not a good idea, but I hit the valve over and over, finally chipped away the paint, and we got it turned off.

He collapsed with sweat pouring off him as we climbed into the truck. He looked at me and said, "When we get back, if they ask you, I want you to tell them you sat in the truck. I would lose my job, and benefits if they ever knew you were in the trenches, because you are not qualified."

I worked at the gas company through my pregnancy. That winter I lived in Sebago, and worked at the gas company in Portland. We had a terrible snow storm, and I was not able to get out of the gulley on route 107. I had to wait for them to open the roads. The Portland office was really upset, but we had an unbelievable amount of snow. My supervisor told me, "You are union, and you are expected to be at the job."

I told her I would do the best I could. It took four tries to get down the road. I finally got to work, and by then the snow had entered Portland, and they closed early, and sent everybody home. However, "You are union and you stay." It was an hour's ride on a good day, and twice as long this day to get home. I quit working there, and worked for Mom and Dad the rest of the winter. That spring I started building the house on the Sandy Beach Road.

Carl Harmon was the contractor, and I was his right hand woman. Building the house consumed the entire summer.

I started the paper work to get electricity months earlier. It went on for a long time, and I still didn't have power. Finally, I called the Central Maine Power supervisor on the phone, and found out the gentlemen I had been working with never did anything with it. One of the advantages in working for Northern Utilities was I had learned about the Public Utilities Commission.

When I got the supervisor for CMP on the line, I said, "I will be calling the PUC as soon as we hang up unless you want to get things rolling." Within an hour I had a call back from Bill Osgood. He and Milton McKeen were going to come to the house in Sebago so I could sign the easement papers they needed. I made an appointment to do the paper work at five-thirty when Gary arrived from work.

They were not at my house at five-thirty. I was boiling, and by the end of the evening I had chewed them into little pieces, and spit them out.

It was way into the construction process before we actually had power. We moved in Labor Day, and I realized I needed a job.

Central Maine Power Company

I checked the Bridgton News, and found Central Maine Power was hiring. I didn't know if I dared to apply, but I thought, why not, maybe they won't remember me. I put in an application, and received a call back for an interview.

When I arrived, it was not either of the men I had chewed out about the line extension. That was good. It was a lady, and we went through the process. It was only a part time job, but that was okay. We finished and she said, "In my eyes you will be perfect for the position, but I want to get the supervisor you will be reporting to."

She stepped out, and came back with Bill Osgood following her into the room. We sat down and he said, "It's you again." Well, I almost died, "I have a couple routine questions. The last question I have to ask you is: You will be working with men on a lot of the jobs. Do you have a problem standing your ground?" He never finished the sentence when he said, "That was stupid of me to even ask. You have the job. You start tomorrow."

I was working in the line department dispatching crews. Then I went out front as the cashier, then I started reading meters, and then I was promoted to the utility worker's position of ordering and stocking poles, transformers, and other supplies. In the winter it was my responsibility to shovel out all of the doors, and make sure everything was okay. On storm situations I worked as a bird-dog. (A bird-dog rides with a crew to show them locations, and is able to communicate with headquarters in case it is necessary. I had a bag of knitting ready to go.)

The qualification of a utility worker was to go out on a line-truck, but they didn't want to give me the training I needed. So, I lost the chance at the job. I stayed on, and asked to be trained repeatedly. So, to appease me they handed me some videos and booklets and said, "This is what you need to know."

I studied the material. We had a storm situation, and the linemen didn't come in. My phone rang, and I went in. I ended up going out on a line-truck with Terry. I had already spent a lot of time listening, and asking lots of questions. Terry and I worked great together. When we left it was thundering and raining. We took care of the downed wire on Route 302 in Raymond, caused by a tree blown over. We were soaked to the bone. The next pole was in Casco. We took off for there, and as we went up in elevation it turned to snow. We found a broken pole. Two of the men went back to get a pole. While they were gone, I looked at Terry and said, "I'll be with you in three minutes."

He said, "What are you going to do?"

"I'm not working in these soaked clothes, I am going to change."

He looked at me and said, "What?"

"I have dry clothes with me and I will be back in three minutes." I stripped off all my wet things except for my bra and panties, even my socks. I dressed in my warm dry clothes. I took my wet things to the truck and hung them over the visor, on the mirror, the steering wheel, the shifting lever, wherever I could, because the truck was running, and the heat was on full bore.

If I got wet again, I'd have dry clothes to wear. I am happy as a pig in shit, because I am wearing dry clothes. Life is good. We changed the pole, and activated the power.

When Terry jumped into the truck he ran head first into my drying clothes. He said, "Holy shit, this has never happened to me before!"

I jumped in, grabbed all my clothes and said, "I am really sorry." The clothes were pretty much dry by now.

Before the storm was over, I probably could have sold the dry clothes at least three times, whether they fit the guys or not. They didn't care, THEY WERE DRY. It was a long hard storm.

One time I set a pole myself. This was before Cookie and I were a couple. I was out on storm damage and Cookie said, "Dee you're going to run the digger truck, you're going to set this pole." I told him I didn't know anything about it, but he was such a patient teacher. He walked me through the whole process, and the guys thought it was great. I was scared to death, but I set that pole, and was pretty excited. I loved that job.

We had a horrific ice storm. It was BRUTAL. We were working from four in the morning until ten at night. We had no power. I kept the wood stoves going, but couldn't take a shower. I was getting four hours sleep at night and then I went back to work to do it all over again. On the seventh day we finally had the power on at the house, but by then I was already at work. At that point they had me out front doing mostly customer service, because I understood how the lines fed, where the men were, and what they were doing, so I could talk with people and square them away.

I had a couple from Brownfield that were on a three-phase line, which means there are three feeds on that road. One of the three feeds had major damage. We were trying to get power to as many people as we could, and then go back to the places needing really extensive work. These people happened to be on this bad line, and the gentleman was verbally abusive. He kept going on and on, and then he looked at me and said, "It is apparent to me that you don't give a rat's ass about us at all."

This is when I lost it. Here I was at day seven. The hat was having trouble covering the dirty hair. I was completely exhausted, and this guy just pushed me over the edge. I looked at him and said, "Look here Mister, this elbow is the only part of me that has not been chewed. If you want it, have at it, if not excuse me a minute, I have to go to the ladies room and have a cry." Before I went to the ladies room I looked at him and said, "I have been here for seventeen hours a day for seven days now. I prefer to be home to make sure I am not losing the meat in my freezer, and my pipes are not frozen. If I didn't care about you, I wouldn't be here. It is very hurtful when you say that to me."

About then my voice started cracking, and I said, "Excuse me; I will be back in a minute." I had a quick cry, and as I went back to talk with him I witnessed his wife beating him with her purse. When I returned I looked at them and said, "I am sorry I broke down."

He looked at me and said, "I'm sorry, I was a fucking ass, I will not bother you again."

I said, "We are doing the best we can."

We had another storm that was a corker. We had crews from as far away as Canada and South Carolina come to help us. They loaded the line-trucks onto military planes, and flew them into Brunswick. They opened the nose of the plane, and out drove the line-trucks ready to go to work.

We had eight or nine trucks from Rhode Island. I went in at six o'clock to bird-dog. All of their men were standing in a circle. Our line supervisor said, "We have bird-dogs for you, two trucks per bird-dog, and this is where we are going to send you." He started introducing the bird-dogs.

Their supervisor, said, "That's fine, however, that bird-dog," and he pointed to me, "I need to pick the two that go with her." That crew had some rough naughty, naughty people. He picked two great men for my team. Anyway, I forged a huge bond with these guys. I was with Cookie when the ice storm of 1998 hit. Cookie received one of the first calls; he had the line-truck at home, and the trouble was in Sebago. When I woke up to the phone ringing I heard what was going on outside. I immediately filled everything in the house with water, the bathtub, pans, pails, and jars. I called Cookie an hour and one-half later. He does not swear, and all he said to me was, "My dear we are f----ed." And that was it.

I said, "Be safe," and I hung up the phone. After that all I heard was crash, crash, crash. It was thirty-six hours before he came home the first time. He had to cut his way up the road. I could not have gone anywhere if I had tried. That evening I heard the chain saw down the road, so I knew Cookie was cutting his way home. I climbed out of bed, and did the best I could to reach him. He positioned the line-truck on the last little hill before our driveway so the headlights shined on the downed trees. He was cutting the downed trees when suddenly; the line-truck disappeared back down the road. It took over four hours to the get the truck back on the road, and up over the hill into the drive. I don't think he slept that night. The next day I called Gary and said, "You have to come get the kids, because I have to go to work." It took us three different attempts on different roads before we could even get close. When we did meet, the kids were passed over a tree downed across the road. So, off to work I went. That was brutal. It was a storm that did not pass; it just sat over us with the drizzle freezing upon contact. We were putting in seventeen hour days, and by day three, we were worse off than day one. Everyone was so defeated. You could clear a line, and when you went back to energize it, something else had come down. It was a very hard storm on everyone.

    We were okay until they opened the schools. Gary didn't live in the same district, how was I going to get my kids back to school? I went to management and asked if I could cut back on the hours, and get the kids and some normalcy back in our lives. I was told, "No, it's your job, and you are expected to do it."

    I didn't know what I was supposed to do. I talked with Cookie and he said, "They don't appreciate what you do, so give your notice."

    I looked at Cookie and I said, "Excuse me, it will be a cold day in hell before I live off any man."

    He said, "I know." And that was it. Cookie told me the most important job a woman will ever do is to raise her children, so that was what I was supposed to do. Well, that kind of sat me back because they are not his children, and yet he wanted to give me that opportunity. I was able to be here for the kids, be baseball and basketball coach, go to their games, and things I could never have done if I was working full time.

I gave my notice, and I started substitute teaching at Sebago for some income. At the same time we were building the shop, and I was trying to build up my stained-glass inventory. I was told I had to have my fingerprints taken. My fingertips were a mess from working on stained glass, sanding, and varnishing.

The first thing the police officer did was look at my fingertips, and then he gave me a lotion, to apply. I didn't think anything of it. One of the officers came and sat beside me; he started asking questions. He finally asked, "What did you do to your fingertips?" I explained what was going on and he said, "Oh, stained glass. You're going to get rich?"

I said, "No it is not about getting rich it's about supporting my habit." That was the wrong choice of words. I meant my habit of being an addicted craft-a-holic, not my habit of being addicted to drugs." Immediately, I was inundated by five people, and at this point, the naïve, little, Hiram-girl saw the light. I looked at these people and said, "Are you kidding me?"

He said, "Let's go take your fingerprints; if they are too scratched and we can't recognize…"

I interrupted and said, "So, if some little boy goes home, and tells his mommy somebody touched his peepee, then it is me. Come on?" They finally took my fingerprints, and lead me out the door. By this time I had been working with the cub scouts and boy scouts. I would never harm a child. It kind of struck me funny, but I guess in this world, you just don't know.

We continued construction of the shop, and I had a couple years to increase the inventory. I produced knitting, crocheting, sewing, and other miscellaneous crafts plus the stained glass. We didn't know what was going to happen. It was very apparent; once I opened the shop the demand was for glass work. I had no room to work on the stained glass at the shop.

It was difficult, because each day I went home, fixed dinner, Cookie cleaned up, and I went to the basement to cut and solder glass, and then carried the pieces to the shop. Three years later we proceeded with expansion of the shop, and I had an area to cut glass, and was able to teach classes on stained glass.

Terry

Terry was unique, and made her mark on the world the minute she was born. In a thundering rain storm she decided not to wait until we arrived at the hospital to be born. We did find shelter at a friend's home.

Terry was an athlete even before she was born, doing somersaults many times. This resulted in the cord being wrapped around her neck three times. Skillfully, Doc untangled the cord. The next problem was finding something so Doc could tie the cord. I remembered I had put a sample of a new invention, made to replace cord tie, in my pocket book. It was a heavy plastic clamp, and we used it. The hospital called in many obstetrical physicians to see this phenomenon. Excitement grew, and soon all hospitals were using this ground breaking invention, but Terry was the first. To see the picture check www.modomed.com

Terry was about three months old, and I had to make a rushed trip to Portland. I could not leave her home because I was nursing her. I took John along, so he could sit in the car with her while I made the flying trip into the store. John was making a face, and was not happy when I returned to the car. Terry had messed her diaper running up her back, down her legs, and oozing through the blanket. In my haste, I forgot to bring a diaper bag. What was I to do? I went to the hospital and headed for the obstetrical floor. Recognizing a nurse I knew I said, "I haint never had no young'uns before and dint know I twas posed to bring diapers wit me." She roared as she handed me a disposable diaper. I had never seen one of them before, and never used one since.

Diane found three-years-old Terry, in the bathroom applying lipstick without the use of a mirror. Scotte joined them, and encouraged her to use more lipstick. "You look like a clown, go show Mama."

Patients were in the waiting room as she came down stairs, and showed everyone her masterpiece saying, "See I'm a clown." I refuse to tell you what happened next. I don't want to be in trouble with the law.

It was clear to see we had an inquisitive, adventurous child; one day I found her inside the cereal cupboard above the refrigerator. She was able to scale to this great height, but could not figure out how to get down, so she opened a box of cereal, and had a snack.

She was mentally inquisitive also. Before she was five, she asked, "Is your brain thinking even when you aren't thinking? Who thought to start with one?" One evening she came to me with a very perplexing problem. She was watching a program on television about evolution. She said, "If this is true, then Adam and Eve can't be true." Now, I had the problem. I don't remember how I helped this little one, but fifty years later she confessed to me she really hoped she had come from a monkey.

One evening she crawled out of bed, and quietly snuck downstairs. Her dad pointed his finger at her, and before he could speak she said, "You don't want me to wake them other kids, do you?" She walked over to her daddy's chair, curled up in his arms, and confessed, "I'm my daddy's little monster!"

Terry was dragged to her sisters' dancing lessons. She was too young for lessons, but the teacher needed her for the recital. Her costume was a replica of the one worn by a teenaged dancer. She was placed on a box, and stood there terrified. The music started, and the older girl began her dance. The song rang out BABY TAKE A BOW, and on cue Terry took a deep bow. She continued to take a bow every time it was sung in the song.

Terry gave the best parties of all the neighborhood kids. She was known as the "hostess with the mostess." Even adults sought her out for help. She spent days making mud pies, searching the mountain for berries and nuts to decorate her pastries. They set on the porch in the sun for days to harden. Some of the berries probably were poisonous, because the birds would not eat them.

One birthday party that was a huge success had everyone, including the boys, making clothespins dolls, and dressing them with scraps of cloth and ribbons. They were having so much fun I had to open the second bag of clothespins. The cake and punch were delayed until all the clothespins were completed.

Tooth Fairy

All of you have had experiences with the tooth fairy. Our tooth fairy was not very diligent, conscientious, or attentive; she let her work slide. She was on time for her first visit; I think she was trying to make an impression. Billy was excited when he found a shiny dime under his pillow the next morning.

Let me tell you about the Tooth Fairy that stopped by the Barnes' household. She definitely was from the depression era. She thought ten cents was still the going rate. She must have been getting a bit senile as she had trouble keeping track of the six children; she was always late. The Barnes' children held a meeting to address this problem. They felt if they had to pay a late fee at the library, for not returning their books on time, then they would initiate a late fee against the Tooth Fairy.

They wanted to keep it simple so as not to stress her aged brain. They asked me to write a note to her saying: "I know you are busy, but we feel you should pay us double, and then double it again each day you are late."

This got the Tooth Fairy's attention and she became more prompt. It took her several years to increase her offering to a quarter.

One day they found a note under the pillow. It read, "Thank you for being patient with this exhausted soul. As a reward to you, my special children, I am going to compensate you like no one else. I will not confiscate your tooth, but leave it for you as a reminder to be kind to your elders."

Childhood

What are some stories you remember of your childhood?

One April day we had a fast warm-up. The ground was still frozen, the snow melted rapidly, and the river rose to near flood stage. The field in front of our house became a pond. Together all of us kids carried the canoe to this pond. As a seven year old, I was getting bored just paddling in a circle, so I stood up and jumped into the water. My all-seeing parents spotted this maneuver, and I was called to the house and chastised.

I never had a bicycle. Everybody in Hiram had a bicycle, but I had to run to keep up with them. So if we were headed to school, I started ahead of them. I would yell, "Okay, I'll meet you there." I ran every place. Occasionally, I borrowed a bicycle lying in the yard for one of my adventures.

I found out a girl on the other side of town got a new bicycle, and just like my family, she passed her bike down to her younger sister. I asked if I could buy the younger sister's old bicycle.

They wanted ten dollars. I was in the fourth grade, and had some money saved. I went to mother, and asked for a list of chores I could do to earn enough money to buy the two-wheeler. Now, I could belong to the group.

Terry told of one of the bike trips with her sisters:

We were going to bicycle down the River Road, and mother reminded us, "No swimming." I guess I couldn't hear very well. It was a very hot day, and we stopped below the falls where there was this small pool of water, like a bathtub. We stripped down to our panties, and went into the pool. We dried off the best we could, and got dressed. No one would know, but my hair went into tight ringlets when it was wet.

When we came home Mother said, "I see you've been swimming!"

"No I haven't."

"Look at the ringlets on the back of your hair."

My sisters said, "We knew we should have left her at home."

Butterscotch Ice Cream

I want to tell a story where Terry rescued all of us.

It was a hot Saturday in the summer. The girls had an early morning appointment at the orthodontist. After Dr. Osher finished tightening bands, and all the other work he did in their mouths, we went grocery shopping. I spotted a sign saying, "Butterscotch Royal Ice Cream on Sale". That was my favorite ice cream. As a kid I used to walk three blocks out of my way to get a cone mounded high with butterscotch royal ice cream, for five cents. Today I was going to relive my childhood. I pushed the grocery buggy to the aisle where they had the paper plates to buy some plastic spoons. I was out of luck; there were none left. I paid for the groceries, and put them in the car dreaming of digging into the box of ice cream immediately. I tried to think of a store that would have plastic spoons. The only place was Kentucky Fried Chicken. I pulled into their parking lot, jumped out of the car, rushed through the door, spotted the spoons, and nonchalantly picked up four spoons. I felt so guilty that I stepped to the counter, and ordered a box of assorted pieces of chicken.

The smell of the chicken demanded immediate attention. The ice cream could wait. The four of us each grabbed a piece of chicken, and started eating. It was so good. One of the girls grabbed the bag of potato chips from the grocery bag, and we all indulged. It was heavenly, and we were starved, so we each had another piece of chicken. With the first course nestled snuggly in our tummies we opened the half gallon of ice cream. Each of us held a spoon in our hand, and as soon as the lid was lifted the spoons dove in. It was a warm day, so the ice cream was soft. After several spoonsful we slowed down, and we hadn't even eaten half of it. I urged them to eat more. They looked at me with cheeks puffed out, and I too felt a bit nauseous.

Terry, the youngest girl, took command; she grabbed the box of ice cream, closed the lid, and put it under the seat saying, "The dogs will love the rest of this when we get home." We were relieved that she put us out of our misery.

For years all anybody had to say was butterscotch royal ice cream, and there was instant nausea. I could eat a bowl of it now, but I don't think I could talk my girls into joining me.

SCHOOL

Connie Kendall Wood volunteered as a gym teacher once a week, and she loved the Hiram girls, because we were ready to run, hop, skip, and jump through hoops. She worked with us on all kinds of gymnastics, cartwheels, and square dancing in grade school. She did the very first track and field event with us, and I won many of the races. We had the Presidential Awards, and I remember in the fifth grade, I succeeded in every event except the half mile. They let me run it again, and when I was victorious I received my Gold Presidential Patch.

I did not want to be involved in dance or music, but Mother had other ideas. I took organ lessons, but did not enjoy practicing. Even though my brothers and sisters and I played together, we lead individual lives as we matured. There was one way I wanted to be like my sisters. I wanted a silver bowl with my name engraved on it, and to get this I had to have some music. My compromise was I would be part of the percussion section of the band. I knew how to read notes, so I played the glockenspiel, and xylophone. It was fun making noise with the tambourine and triangle, and dancing to the rhythm.

I knew my passion was sports. I begged my mother to let me quit band. I told her, "I will run every race, play every sport, but please no music." We were not allowed to quit anything, but I was allowed to take a leave of absence from band. I had to work extra hard to achieve the points. I had to run for class offices, student council, maintain honor grades, etc. I lived in the shadow of my two older sisters in everything I did except sports. I excelled in sports. I also received my engraved silver bowl when I graduated.

My love of field hockey started when I was in the sixth grade. Scotte was a sophomore, and I went to practice with her. I beg to stay and watch. I sat there wiggling and jiggling, and the coach said, "Would you like to run with the girls?" I ran with them, and then she said, "Would you like to pick up a stick?" In the sixth grade, I was actually practicing with the high school girls. I was so excited when the coach said, "Would you like to keep a stick, and take it home with you?" That was the beginning of the love of field hockey. I made the varsity field hockey team my freshman year of high school, and also in college.

In softball, I could catch, but couldn't throw. I wasn't a good hitter, but the coach worked with me, and I became good at bunting, and because I could run so fast I could get to first base, and then steal all the bases and score. I played an aggressive guard in basketball, ran track, and any other sport that time allowed.

Terry tells this story that I had never heard.

John let me drive the car when I was in the fourth grade. He came to the Baldwin school to pick us up, and he decided it was time I learned how to drive, because I kept asking him, "What are you doing now? What is that for? What did you just do?"

John sputtered, "Will you just be quiet? I guess you need to learn how to drive."

I answered, "I can't drive; I can't even touch the pedals."

"Oh, you will." He dropped everyone else off, and then he drove to Shotgun Alley. He put me behind the wheel, and told me what to do. I drove to the end, stopped, and he turned the car around, and I drove back again. He threatened he would never pick me up again if I ever told anyone about driving.

I never had much of a chance to drive the doodlebug. I was the youngest, and was always the passenger. They told me I couldn't drive until I could start the engine by pulling the cord.

Don Silvia was the instructor for Drivers Ed. One of the girls in our group was from a very poor family, and they did not have a shower. They probably did not have running water in the house. I think I talked with mother about this girl, and she said there were stories about sexual abuse in the family, and possibly she did not bathe as a means of protecting herself. Mr. Silvia always reminded us in class to shower and use deodorant, but she didn't hear him, so one day another girl and I took her aside. We asked her if she could get to school early. She told us she could, so we asked her to bring a clean set of clothes, and we went with her, and showed her how the showers worked, and stayed with her. The last two times we drove she came early. The instructor let her drive first, and then we let her out at her house. He delivered lots of students to their homes. They don't do that anymore.

I was in the eighth grade, and went to hoop camp in Farmington. It was a really great experience for me. It was the first time I went off alone, and did not have to compete with my sisters. I guess you knew I would never be a ballerina or beauty queen, but I loved sports. I met some nice girls from Gray/New Gloucester that lived on a farm. I found people that could understand my way of life. I loved the college at Farmington. It was in the mountains in the middle of the town, not a whole separate campus.

Being the baby of the family, I always found myself wiggling my way into my older sisters' life. Of the four Musketeers, Terry McClare had her driver's license. Diane's class was going to have Senior. Skip Day. Denise,Mo, and I convinced Terry Mac she should drive us to Old Orchard Beach. We struck up a conversation with this young man with a camera. He spoke to the kids on the beach, "Oh, this is Senior Skip Day, come on gather everyone around for a picture." We made a pyramid and Diane was at the top.

We didn't know he was a photographer for the newspaper. The next day there was a huge picture titled "Sacopee Students Skip School". Diane was called into the superintendent's office; and he said, "Diane, you are a smart girl, and the president of the student council. Why weren't you smart enough to say you were from Bonney Eagle?" The superintendent's son was kneeling in the front row.

You taught us to be honest, and you would not lie for us. You made me go to school the day of our senior skip day. I had a note from you which read, "Terry has my permission to leave school." They would not accept the note, and we had to serve a detention. We did the crime, we'll pay the time.

We went to the detention room, and Mr. Lord came to the door and said, "Excuse me; I need to see both Terrys in my office." We stood up to leave, and he said, "Get your things."

I thought, oh boy, what is going to happen to us now? We followed him trembling, and then he said, "I need someone to solicit door to door for Dollars for Scholars, and you two are the only ones I can actually count on to do the job."

Terry Mac said, stuttering, "I can't knock on the door, and asks them for money."

I said, "You've got the wheels, I've got the knowledge." We were all set; it was great. I made her get out of the car, and stand next to me. We returned to school at four o'clock, and handed several hundred dollars to Mr. Lord with the receipts.

The second time we had a detention was when we went to Mac's house. We didn't think anyone would figure it out. They called my mother to see if I was at home. She told them, "No she went to school."

"She isn't here."

Mother asked, "Is Terry Mac at school?"

"No."

"Well, they are together, go get them." They called Mac's house, and her step-brother was numb enough to answer the phone. The jig was up. We had to serve detention for that one too. Larry pulled us out of the detention room; he needed flowers for an awards banquet that evening. We drove to Steep Falls, picked up the flowers, returned, and arranged them on the tables.

The year I broke my finger playing softball I had to literally sit in study hall instead of going to the cafeteria where the honor roll students could study. I had failed French, because the teacher couldn't read my writing, because of my broken finger. It was the worst study hall ever. So, Mac and I with a bunch of boy losers were raising heck. Mr. Silvia had had it and he issued a summons for the five of us. "You will not report to this study hall, you will come to my room for fun and games." We were all excited about fun and games. We enter his room, and he sat with his dictionary open. If you can spell all of the words in the dictionary between fun and game, then detention is over. You can be out of here in a minute."

"Cool, all right!"

"Fun."

"F-u-n."

The teacher continued reading the list for our response, "functional, fundus, fungal, fungi, fungicide,"

We never made it out of the F's. Spelling was not my strong suit, and Terry Mac and the boys could not spell at all.

Jobs

I asked Terry to tell me about some of her jobs.

My first job was selling puppies when I was about ten-years-old. Suzy-Q was going to have puppies. I was excited, but Mother was not exactly pleased about it. Mother said, "If you sell those puppies you may keep one of them. There were six puppies at ten dollars each or fifty dollars, because my puppy was free. That was a lot of money.

I took out my crayons, and started making flyers and posters. I had to get out there and sell the puppies. Connie, the organ teacher, bought one of the puppies. I was young enough that I had no shame in pestering the patients. Finally, they were all sold, and I had my own puppy to love.

Blueberry picking was my next job. The time I remember best was the time you left us girls at Upton, so we could pick berries. On Thursday and Sunday you and Dad came to Upton, and gathered the blueberries we had, and took them home to sell. Fred, the store owner, came to check on us. Our job besides picking was to go out in the field, and charge people that came to pick. We picked all day, and cleaned the berries at night. Diane made more money than I did because she was a faster picker. That summer we made close to three hundred dollars. We divided the money from the pickers, and then we kept track of what we each picked. Mother delivered the berries to different customers, and put some in the waiting room for patients to buy. We started out selling them for $1.00, and then the next year we asked $1.50. We whined about it, and we decided to ask $2.00 a quart.

When my sisters were older they passed their weed pulling jobs to me. I didn't like weeding, and the jobs didn't last long.

The next job was working at the Fryeburg Nursery where they grew small seedlings. It was April vacation. My two sisters, two neighbor boys, and I worked this job. We were given lengths if twine which we hooked to our belt. We climbed onto a wagon which took us to the field. A machine went through the field to loosen the trees. We pulled out the trees that were 10 inches or taller, counted to make sure we had twenty-five in a bunch. They taught us how to wrap and tie the bunch. We laid them out in the rows, and covered the roots. Later a truck came out to the field, they took a bundle, dipped the roots in a pail of water and lay them on a pallet. Then the full pallets were taken to the packing house.

The first day we all went to the field, we stuck very close to each other. The next day they put Scotte in the packing house, and four of us were in the field. We felt like we were the slaves starring in the movie "Roots". I realized that out of all the workers in the field, Scotte had the highest education, a sophomore in high school.

I was in the eighth grade and I decided I wanted to get a higher education, than the field hands. Either Sam or Scotte convinced the boss all of us should be in the packing house. For the final three days we all worked in the packing house, which was still pretty much slave labor. When I came home the first night I told Mother, "I really learned something today." My mother thought I was going to tell her I learned the difference between a spruce and cedar tree. Instead I said, "I learned to study like hell, because I don't want to do that the rest of my life."

I want to say, "Thanks Mom for putting me through this, because I really learned I wanted to get a better education." Even as an eighth grader I realized the only reason these men were working there was because they had no education. It certainly was a wonderful lesson for all of us kids. At the end of the week it was WOW, when we received a check for a hundred dollars. I never made that much money before.

I worked cleaning cottages with Erika for two summers, and a couple summers with my sisters. I found out when people were on vacation, they were not clean. They did not wipe their feet at the door. I made about $30.00 a day at that job. I remember being interviewed at Jordan Reality. They said, "Oh, you're Margaret's daughter, ok, I don't care how old you are. I know you will do a good job. Erika had the car and I had a job.

Mother did a good job asking us what we were interested in, and not telling us what we had to do. The guidance counselor asked me what I wanted to be and I said, "A cow girl, I don't know." I knew I enjoyed being in the garden with my mother. I liked growing, and working with plants. Mother asked me if I had thought about working at the flower shop. I loved growing things. I thought that was something I could be interested in.

Mother coached me, but would not speak for me. We walked into the florist shop, and she introduced me to Larry, and then stepped back. She made me speak for myself. He immediately let me know he did not want any high school kids. He kept shaking his head no. I just kept talking. "I am not asking you to hire me; I want to be like an intern. You will not have to pay me, I want to find out if this is the career I want to pursue. I want to see how the business works."

"I want to volunteer. Did you hear me? I am doing this for nothing." Pretty soon his head was going in circles until he was nodding yes.

"Oh, so you are willing to come here, and give up your Saturday's?"

"Sure unless I have a game."

"Okay, you can come to work on Saturday."

I swept the floor, trimmed the stems, and took care of the flowers that arrived, etc. If I saw a florist making a bow, I did not feel guilty if I stopped sweeping, and watched to learn; after all I wasn't being paid. When Larry was out of the shop delivering or whatever, the designers explained what they were doing, or what they wanted to achieve and said, "Now Terry, I want you to start putting the greens this way, and then they would finish the floral piece. They taught me how to make ribbon bows, and they sat me down and told me to make six red bows like this, and then make ten white bows. Larry did not realize that at times I was actually doing the designing. The ladies took me under their wings.

I insisted Todd, my boyfriend, order my prom corsage from this florist shop. When the order came in, I basically made my own corsage. I was out on deliveries when Todd came to pick up the corsage, and Larry did not know who he was; he charged him full price. I was so upset; I wanted to quit. I said to my mother, "I will not work for this man anymore! I am done."

She said, "You will go to work tomorrow because Sunday is Mother's Day, and you never kick a man when he is down. You will go to work and work as hard as you can, and then at the end of the day I do not care what you say to him. Be respectful, but you can let him have it, and let him know how you feel." I went in that day, and he met me at the door. He said, "Miss Barnes, here is your time-card, and that is a time-clock. I want you to punch in from now on. You are hired."

"I'm going to get paid?"

"Yes, you're going to keep your time-card, and you are going to be paid." It was about five years before I told Larry the story about the corsage and he was aghast. "Why didn't you tell me? I would have given the money back to you."

I used to bring home crippled flowers and things from the trash barrel to practice designing arrangements.

Larry talked with me about Rittners School of Floral Design in Boston. We looked into it and you asked me where I was going to stay, etc. Buddy must have overheard it, and was telling his boss at the concrete company. They had friends from Boston that had a camp on Moose Pond just down the road from their house.

Dave talked with them, and told them I was looking for a place to stay. Buddy took me to meet them, and they agreed to take me in. That is how the connection was made. Sunday night they stopped at the house, and I got in the car with their three boys, and we headed for Massachusetts. They lived in Stoneham. That evening they gave me a key to their house, and said, "You can take the train to the school in Boston."

I looked at them and said "I have no idea how to get into Boston".

"You take the "T"."

"What's the T? I don't even know."

"Here, sit down and we'll show you. You go one block this direction, turn right and then go two blocks, and then turn left until you find the loading sign, which wasn't far away." The first morning Dad drove me to the station, and I got on the T. He said, "Take the orange line, get out at Malden square, and then get on the green line and take it to another place."

"Yeah, okay." I had no idea what he meant.

The first morning, I will never forget, I am smiling at people and saying "Good morning," and they are not smiling back. So, I figured they were not smiling people. I got on the T and got off at North Station, which was a very scary place. I didn't know how to find, or how to get onto the green line. I was walking, scared half to pieces, and out the door I went. When I realized I was not supposed to go out the door, I turned to go back, but the door was locked. There was a "street person" standing there mocking me, "You can't get back in there, Ha Ha Ha." I was terrified; I turned and ran up the steps, and went up onto the street. I was kind of waiting patiently as I watched the stairs out of the corner of my eye. Pretty soon up came a nice lady and I said, breathlessly, "Excuse me, I am from Maine and I have never been in a train station. I am supposed to be getting on the green line. I came out a door, and I don't know how to get back in the station."

"Oh, Sweetie Pie, you have to cross the road, and go through that door."

"Oh, all right, thank you so much. Be seeing you." I went over there, and I tried to walk right through thinking I had already paid my fare.

"Hey, lady you have to pay."

Scared, but determined I said, "I already paid when I got on."

He replied, "But you left and re-entered."

"Okay."

I finally arrived at my destination, and then I had to walk three blocks to the school. Riding the T in the morning was really crazy and crowded. The second morning I met a young lady, and we stayed together; we met again the third morning. We didn't necessarily wait for each other, but it was nice when we did see each other. She gave me a lot of little hints, like always have a book with you.

Coming home I had to carry the flowers I designed that day. I got on the train, and some young boys were harassing me. I was carrying these flowers, and probably did not look like I belonged in Boston, and these young boys started to follow me in the train station. When I went downstairs where there were more people, I turned around and said, "Look, I am from Maine, and I am a survivor, and I will do whatever it takes to survive. I can run fast, kick hard, punch, bite, and dig. Which would you prefer?" All the time I had the flowers in my hand and my insides were trembling.

They mumbled, "We were just checking you out."

"You are rude and mean, now, go away" And it was sweet to hear a couple claps from the people around me. "Yea! Good for you."

I attended school for six weeks.

Their swimming pool in the back yard was so inviting after the hot train ride home from the city. After I cooled down, from a leisurely swim, I went to the house, and sat the table for supper. If I knew what was planned for supper I would start the preparations. I tried to be of help, and did the dishes after the meal.

They were not coming to Maine one weekend, so I drove the Maverick to Massachusetts. Mother let me take the car because you knew I wouldn't be out at night, because the lights did not work.

Accident

The florist shop had to deliver several poinsettias to St. Joseph's Academy by a certain time for decoration. "Quick, quick Miss Barnes, hurry up. Take the Boundary Road."

The sun was shining on the road on the way over, but by the time I came home the sun was gone leaving the narrow road covered with a sheet of ice. I was an inexperienced driver, and I was hurrying to get back, because I had a basketball game.

Mother arrived at the shop just as a customer reported the accident to Larry. When I saw mother coming, I thought, oh boy, I am going to get it now. She showed me where I put on the brakes, the whole time I was denying it. While she was talking with me a man stepped up and said, "Don't be too hard on her. My dad and I just hit each other. The road is very icy." The ledges are still there, but they have widened the road.

We were late for the basketball game, but Mother talked with the coach and explained what happened, and asked him to let me play to work out the stress of the day. The first thing I did when I went on the floor was to wipe out a girl. The official yelled, "You're out! I am not going to have anyone play like that." That was when the coach pulled the official aside, and explained everything that had happened. "You have got to let this girl play." They both told me to calm down.

Floral Design

A renowned horseman from the area died, and the florist shop was asked to do a floral arrangement. The designers were going to make a horse shoe. In my mind I could see a horse's head. I took a piece of paper, and started sketching, erasing, and sketching again. I redid the horse's muzzle, sketched and erased. I sketched it onto a piece of Styrofoam. All the time I was envisioning the flowers I would use. I could use the spider mums to give fullness to the mane, dye another spider mum dark, and cut it in half for the eyelashes.

Larry took the arrangement to the funeral home, and another florist said to Larry, "This has your card on it, but you didn't do this; it is not your style. You must have new designer."

"Oh, that would be Miss Barnes," Larry said.

"Would she like another job?" the other florist asked.

"You can't have her; she's mine."

Egg princess

Mother roped me into the Egg Princess contest. I could not figure out why, because I never thought of myself as a pretty girl. Mother coaxed, "Five hundred dollars toward your college tuition." That got my attention. Mother told me that Grandpa

Barnes' ancestors were from Pittsfield, Maine, where they held the contest, and then I agreed to do it. I entered it for two years. The first year I went to Limerick to an egg farm, because they were going to sponsor me. Mother said, "I made an appointment for you. This is the address, go and find it." It was a good experience, because I knew nothing about the egg industry. I walked into this rotten egg factory, and talked with some of the workers. Again, I realized the importance of an education because these workers were not highly educated.

The contest was really interesting. The first year it was only to answer questions, and then they added talent the second year. I said, "I have no talent, Mom. I can't sing like Diane."

I finally ended up doing a floral design. I picked all kinds of wild flowers from the field, and Dad helped me create a birch bark basket. I wanted it to be all natural.

The most fun was making an omelet in the world's largest frying pan. It was seven feet in diameter. The other exciting thing was Mother showed me the glass hearse that Grandpa drove as a teenager. He delivered a body to the adjacent town on a cold, blustery, winter day. He crawled into the hearse to get out of the weather on his return trip home. Another buggy driver saw him sit up to get his bearings, and it scared the buggy driver to death thinking the dead were rising up.

All of my friends thank you, Mom, because I am the best omelet maker ever. They would cheer, "Thank you for being the second runner upper in the Egg Princess Contest."

College

Terry went to college in Farmington, and played field hockey all through college.

She told me the following story: I made the acquaintance of a nice young man after flirting across the room. The next week he stopped me and said, "I think we have to talk." I wondered what was going on.

He said, "When I was home this weekend, I told my mom about meeting you. She told me to ask you what your grandma's name is."

I told him Rose.

He said, "Darn it, we're cousins." That was a bummer, because he was such a nice young man.

Terry taught fourth grade after college, and is still working at the same job. She coached Junior Varsity field hockey, and then she applied for the Varsity field hockey coaching position when it became available, and has been the varsity coach since then.

She has done all of this plus raising three children.

There is not a rotten one in the bunch.

ABOUT THE AUTHOR

Margaret Barnes Heath found great pleasure in interviewing her adult children, and learning stories she had never heard before. There are many more stories yet to be heard, so she will continue to look for them.

In many places she let the children tell their stories directly to you. These stories took place between 1951 thru 2015.

Her children are the apples of her eye.

Margaret has written four previous books about family. *Doc, Me and Family, Hiram by the River, The Country Doctor Who Cared, and She Wore Many Hats.*

Parents Poem
By Scotte E. Barnes

People so seldom
Appreciate the good things in life, but I've
Realized how lucky I am to have
Evolved from people like you.
You never cease to tire for we are your children.
Thank you for bringing me into this world and
Standing by me in times of need
You've opened my eyes and now
I shall see for myself.

We are formed by our families. We are molded by our memories. We are shaped by our successes. We may feel daunted by our destinies, but we must be determined to rarely be dismayed. Our words are like dandelion fluff surfing on a light summer breeze on a journey to nowhere. It is our actions that reflect the true nature of our being.

The flower soon fades away and it is the tiny seed that survives in the damp darkness, patiently waiting for the warmth of a brilliant light to shine upon it and give it new life.

Written by Karen Hawkins

Made in the USA
Columbia, SC
27 November 2023